The Complete Films of SPENCER TRACY

The Complete
Films of

SPENCER TRACY

by DONALD DESCHNER

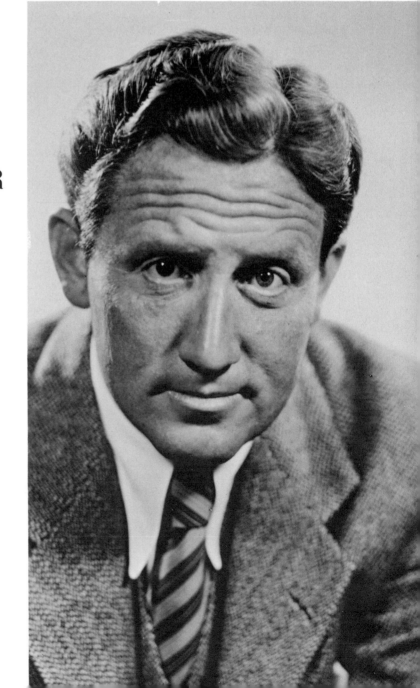

A Citadel Press Book
Published by Carol Publishing Group

I wish to express my gratitude to the following authors and publishers for their permission to quote from their books.

I Blow My Own Horn, by Jesse Lasky with Don Weldon. Copyright © 1957 by Jesse Lasky and Don Weldon.
Reprinted by permission of Doubleday & Company, Inc.

The Wind at My Back, by Pat O'Brien. Copyright © 1964 by Pat O'Brien and Stephen Longstreet.
Reprinted by permission of Doubleday & Company, Inc.

A Portrait of Joan, by Joan Crawford with Jane Kesner Ardmore. Copyright © 1962 by Joan Crawford Steele. Reprinted by permission of Doubleday & Company, Inc.

The Fifty Year Decline and Fall of Hollywood, by Ezra Goodman, Simon and Schuster. Copyright © 1961 Reprinted by permission of Ezra Goodman.

A Special Kind of Magic, by Roy Newquist. Copyright © 1967 by Rand McNally & Company.
Reprinted by permission of Roy Newquist.

D.D.

Acknowledgments

Grateful acknowledgement is made to the many individuals and organizations who aided the author in preparation of this book:

Columbia Pictures Corporation • Metro-Goldwyn-Mayer, Inc. • Paramount Pictures Corporation • Twentieth Century-Fox Film Corporation • United Artists Corporation • Warner Brothers-Seven Arts, Inc. • Mrs. Spencer Tracy • Mrs. Doris Chambers; the John Tracy Clinic • Director's Guild of America • Equity • Aftra • Screen Actor's Guild • Writer's Guild of America, West, Inc. • Cliff McCarty • Colleen Moore • King Vidor • Garson Kanin • Commander Ross, U.S. Coast Guard • American Red Cross • Romano Tozzi • John Wexley • Ezra Goodman • Library and Museum of the Performing Arts, New York City • Free Public Library of Elizabeth, New Jersey • Public Library of Cincinnati and Hamilton Country (Bess Dehner) • New York Public Library • Father Flanagan's Boys Town (Mr. Straka) • U.S. Army Pictorial Center • Allen County Historical Society, Ohio (Joseph Dunlap) • Library — Special Collections, University of California at Los Angeles • Library — Special Collections, University of Southern California • General Services Administration — National Archives, Washington, D. C. • Lima Public Library, Ohio (Frances Burnette) • The Hoblitzelle Theater Arts Library, University of Texas (W. H. Crain) • Library, University of Michigan • County Clerk, Freeport, Illinois • Stanley Kramer Productions (George Glass) • Vitaprint Corp. • U.S. Information Agency • American Cancer Society • Norwood Films • Health Department, City of Milwaukee, Wis. • Ripon College • United Artists Associated • Dore Schary • Dr. J. Clark Graham • William O. Douglas • Ray Thelan • Lillian Schwartz and the staff of the library of the Academy of Motion Picture Arts and Sciences • the staff of the Art and Literature Departments of the Los Angeles Public Library • and the Free Public Library, Trenton, New Jersey (Rebecca Muehleck).

To the following publishers and publications for reprint permissions: *Commonweal* • *Daily Variety* • Ideal Publication Corp. • *Library Journal* • *Look* • *The Nation* • National Board of Review of Motion Pictures, Inc. • *The New Republic* • *Newsweek* • *The New Yorker* • Quigley Publications Co. • *The Saturday Evening Post* • and *Time*. Also the Los Angeles *Times* • New York *Daily News* • New York *Times* • Triangle Publications, Inc. • Trenton *Times* • Lima *News* • and the Milwaukee *Journal*.

For stills: Especially Harvey Stewart, Murray Hill Station, Post Office Box 277, New York, New York 10016 • Adon Studio, Lima, Ohio • Kenneth Lawrence • John Lebold • Gunnard Nelson • Bruco Enterprises • Charles Smith • The Larry Edmunds Book Store • Oliver Dernberger • Ray Stuart • Fred Fehl • Gene Ringgold • Hollywood Book Service • Collector's Book Store • Wayne Martin • W. R. Van Courtland • Myron Braum • Theatre Poster Exchange • and the Cherokee Book Shop.

Contents

The Complete Films of SPENCER TRACY

Introduction

by THE HONORABLE WILLIAM O. DOUGLAS
Associate Justice, United States Supreme Court

Spencer Tracy and I arrived in New York City about the same time, he in March, 1922, and I in September. I met him a few years later at a premiere in New York City when he was on his way up the ladder. A warm friendship was formed instantly. In my SEC days in Washington, D.C. (1934–39) he was in and out of the city, and usually called me. That kind of relationship continued after I went on the Court in 1939. It was a casual friendship, yet extremely intimate. Our correspondence was skimpy. The last time I saw him was when *Judgment at Nuremberg* was being filmed in Hollywood. We had lunch together in the studio.

When he died, I felt as if my twin brother had passed away. There apparently was a likeness between us. I was frequently taken for him in crowds, and some of my friends attached the nickname "Spence" to me on that account. Once, about twenty years ago he appeared in the nation's capital for the premiere of one of his movies. By prearrangement, I waited for him at the rear exit. Many people surged into the dimly lit alley and, taking me for him, asked, "Mr. Tracy, will you give me your autograph?"

I obliged, and several dozen took the forgeries home. The crowd had mostly gone when Spencer appeared, and my account of the episode made him chuckle as we sipped a nightcap in some secluded spot.

I never knew anyone more American than he. I realize that the label "American" means various things, even a "vigilante" to some. But Spencer was the opposite. He was Thoreau, Emerson, Frost. His spectrum of ideas included a wide range; he was no respecter of prejudice; his society was classless except for men and women of talent. To that aristocracy all were welcome.

Therefore one was always at ease with him. He emanated warmth and tolerance. I know he never talked bunk. He thought and talked in simple terms. His values were humanistic.

He was utterly unencumbered by nonsense in his remarkable ability as an actor. He filled the role of Darrow in *Inherit the Wind* as easily as he dressed for an outing. He seldom wore makeup, he told me. He searched for the simple truths out of which great friendships and enduring loves are fashioned.

I once asked a contemporary, who knew him better than I, what was the secret of his stage and screen success. This person replied: "The aim of most artists is to strip away the unessentials—Spence did this. I think that that is why he is so universally admired . . . because . . . hopefully the real truth is universal."

Spencer Tracy in a true sense was on a wavelength with humanity across the globe. He knew the predatory nature of man but searched for the kindlier qualities they also have in common. In that search he developed tolerance and great insights. Because he extolled the virtues that he found in all men, he himself flowered as a human being and became uninhibited and wholly integrated.

Spence was indeed a rare human being—a man for all peoples, all faiths, all seasons.

It was inspiring to play opposite Tracy. His is such simplicity of performance, such naturalness and humor. He walks through a scene just as he walks through life. He makes it seem so easy, and working with him I had to learn to underplay. We worked together as a unit, as if we'd worked together for years. No matter how often you rehearse a scene, when the camera starts turning he surprises you with some intonation or timing so that your response is new and immediate.

> JOAN CRAWFORD
> from her autobiography, *A Portrait of Joan,*
> written with Jane Ardmore, Doubleday & Co., 1964.

What is a good actor? To me Spencer Tracy is a good actor, almost the best. Because you don't see the mechanism working, the wheels turning. He covers up. He never overacts or is hammy. He makes you believe he is what he is playing.

> HUMPHREY BOGART
> as quoted by Ezra Goodman
> in *The Fifty Year Decline and Fall of Hollywood,*
> Simon and Schuster, 1961.

My recollections of Spencer Tracy, indeed, are very pleasant and happy ones. Above all, he was a real professional on the set, always knew his lines and came prepared, and would brook no nonsense when it came to the work itself. Invariably, he took two hours for lunch and went home promptly at five, regardless of the shooting schedule. I recall, too, that he had a delightful sense of humor. For some reason or other, he always enjoyed teasing me, probably because I often rose to the bait. In many ways, he was a private person; taciturn is possibly a good word to describe that quality. I don't remember any special anecdotes, but I do recall one thing that would seem counter to the rough and rugged image he presented on the screen—he was an impeccable dresser, sartorially splendid at all times, and had his clothes tailored by one of the great specialists in New York. One of his most celebrated qualities was an intense power of concentration. One never had the feeling that he was "acting" in a scene, but that the truth of the situation actually was happening, spontaneously, at the moment he spoke his lines. I can recall no particular change in him, professionally or personally, between our two early films (1932) and the later ones (1950-51).

JOAN BENNETT

Film-Making With Spencer Tracy

by STANLEY KRAMER

I can't explain why I was never able to say to him what I wanted to say: that he was a great actor. Everyone else said it a thousand times over, but I never managed it. Once I told him I loved him. That came quite easily, and he believed me and was emotional about it. But I was afraid to say, "Spencer, you're a great actor." He'd only say, "Now what the hell kind of thing is that to come out with?" He wanted to know it; he needed to know it. But he didn't want you to *say* it—just *think* it. And maybe that was one of the reasons he was a great actor. He thought and listened better than anyone in the history of motion pictures. A silent close-up reaction of Spencer Tracy said it all.

Those who know say that nobody—but nobody—could drink or fight or cause more trouble than Tracy in his early days in Hollywood. He came to California out of a smash success on Broadway as Killer Mears in *The Last Mile* and started a one-man rebellion. The studio publicity departments kept a lot more out of the papers than they put in. But he did *Captains Courageous* and *Boys Town* and a lot of other great things. And he looked and behaved like Everyman. Clark Gable was taller and more handsome and more

of a sex symbol, but in *Test Pilot* all the men and half the women in the audience wanted Tracy to get Myrna Loy.

He was full of surprises. He never stopped rebelling, but he did stop drinking. And who could have forecast that the red hair would turn pure white? Or that he would rent a house on a hillside and, instead of going out every night, never go out at all? His intimate friends came to him, a few people at a time, on the hillside where he held court and exchanged gossip and news and conversation: Chester Erskine from *The Last Mile,* the Kanins, Hepburn, Cukor, and the Negulescos from the full years, Abe Lastfogel, his agent. I brought up the rear like a chapter titled "The Last Decade." No matter what play or performance or book might be discussed, nothing could match his insatiable desire for plain gossip. What went on at the Daisy Club was really a fascination. He announced and savored as a choice tidbit each new pairing off of the jet set. I never understood his sources—most of the time I thought he made it all up—but usually he was right.

Spencer Tracy retired from films fourteen times in the last ten years. Before each film he announced his retirement—and then again upon its completion. Somehow I thought these last years were a great "put-on." I mean he put us all "on" because he had become so impatient. Katharine Hepburn said many times that he was much too impatient for the time and place in which he found himself. He was impatient with agents and lawyers and publicity men and reporters and photographers and directors and the whole damned system. He knew he was irritable so he put everybody "on" to cover it. He was ill—on and off—and that didn't help. So he stood under the hot lights and perspired through the extra takes and the technical nuisances. The cameraman would ask for another take, and Tracy would just stare back disgustedly. He *was* disgusted, but he fixed that look so that you knew he would do it again anyhow. He would work now only in modern dress, with no makeup. That meant he could breeze in ready for work with no "nonsense," as he called it. If a makeup man tried to powder-puff his forehead, Tracy would push him away and give him a look as though he were somebody he had just thrown up. The crew came to know those interchanges were really what Tracy enjoyed.

We would always start the film with a closed set. Tracy didn't want a bunch of idiots clambering all over the place. One week later it was like Las Vegas. Everybody was there to see him: bookies, ballplayers, fighters, and press, along with a million actors just there to watch. He loved to get hold of a small press group and disagree with everything asked or said. He'd finally get himself into an indefensible position and then act his way out as though *they* were in the wrong.

Still-photographers drove him crazy. He always said he hated stills, and he pretended that he didn't care by looking down at the ground or turning half away from the camera. Then he'd argue that that was the way people stood or looked naturally. He posed for a hundred thousand stills in his time and claimed none of them ever appeared—"except in the B'nai B'rith *Messenger*."

On the first day of the first picture on which we were associated (*Inherit the Wind*), I asked him to do an additional take on a scene in which he had mumbled the lines. He looked at me for a full minute with the glance that withers. And I mean a full minute—not fifty-five seconds. He was just giving the crew and assorted spectators a chance to quiet down, and then he said: "Mr. . . . Kramer . . . (it took eight seconds to say the Mr. Kramer) . . . It . . . has . . . taken . . . me . . . thirty . . . years . . . to . . . learn . . . how . . . to . . . speak . . . lines. . . . If . . . you . . . or . . . a . . . theater . . . arts . . . major . . . from . . . UCLA . . . want . . . to . . . do . . . this . . . speech . . . I . . . am . . . quite . . . willing . . . to . . . step . . . aside." Then he picked me

Oskar Werner visits with Stanley Kramer, Spencer Tracy, and Katharine Hepburn on the set of Guess Who's Coming to Dinner

Hepburn, Kramer, and Tracy on the set of Guess Who's Coming to Dinner

up, shook me a little, dusted me off, and said: "All right, we ought to try it again." His speech had nothing to do with this particular scene. He was merely indicating that he couldn't stand still for a lot of takes.

During the filming of *Inherit the Wind,* we had Tracy and Fredric March nose to nose for long courtroom battles in dialogue and assorted histrionics. The stage was filled with people from every office and company on the lot. And how these two luxuriated in the applause of the audience. Every take brought down the

house, and their escapades were something to see. March would fan himself vigorously with a large straw fan each time Tracy launched into an oration. Tracy had no props, but he got even. He sat behind March and picked his nose during a three-and-one-half-minute summation.

I think the role of the American judge in the film *Judgment at Nuremberg* was one of Tracy's favorites. He was nominated for an Academy Award and told everyone within hearing that he was voting for Maximilian Schell, the defense attorney in the same film. Tracy would say facetiously, "I just sat there listening and these other fellows did the work." Maybe so, but when he read the last speech in court: "This is what we stand for . . . justice . . . truth . . . and the value of a single human being . . ." I *believed* that was what we stood for, and I won't soon forget how he said it.

Of course, it was impossible to outguess Tracy's attitude or concentration. At one moment he threatened to murder a fellow actor who was nibbling on a pastrami sandwich between takes in one of the courtroom scenes. And he meant it. The following day he played an intensely dramatic scene with Burt Lancaster in a jail cell, and, as he turned to exit, he muttered under his breath to Al Horwitz, the publicist: "Nothing to it, Al. A cinch."

Montgomery Clift was in *Nuremberg.* He was ill—very ill—and it was Tracy who pulled him through. Monty couldn't remember the lines—he was literally going to pieces. Tracy just grabbed his shoulders and told him he was the greatest young actor of his time and to look deep into his eyes and play to him and the hell with the lines. He did, and that saved Monty's life for a little longer because he got an Academy nomination, and he was proud of it.

Spencer Tracy liked Frank Sinatra. I guess it takes one impatient to know another. He would tell with great glee how Sinatra walked off one picture and flew to Rome. Or how he made a company rebuild all its sets in California because he didn't want to go to Madrid. I didn't think it half so amusing as Tracy did, because it had also happened to me. Tracy would complain that he had to play his over-the-shoulder closeups in *Devil at Four O'Clock* with a coat hanger because Sinatra wasn't there. Then he would twinkle and say Sinatra had called him and told him he wanted him for his next picture. I don't think this ever happened, but I do think Spencer Tracy knew that he was Spencer Tracy and could afford the anecdote. He told it once too often, because during the filming of *It's A Mad, Mad, Mad, Mad World,* Phil Silvers must have mentioned to Tracy a hundred times in front of a thousand

Hepburn, Tracy, Houghton, Poitier, and Kramer on the set of Guess Who's Coming to Dinner

people that he would ask for him in his next picture.

During the filming of *Mad World* with all the comedians, I think Spencer Tracy was in poorer health than I could remember: he had bad color and no stamina whatever. But then, even though this lack of energy showed, I think he had his best time ever during the making of a film. The comedians worshiped him. Never before or since has a king had the court full of jesters who strove only to entertain him so that his majesty might say "That was funny," or just laugh or smile. Milton Berle, Jonathan Winters, Buddy Hackett, Phil Silvers, Mickey Rooney—even the silent Caesar—crowded about him and vied for his affection. They had it. And he talked about them to the very last; he loved them all.

Spencer Tracy was one of the most sensitive men I've known. He could be hurt easily by commission and omission. Once, after having finished *Ship of Fools,* I told a British newspaperman that I thought Oskar Werner was as fine an actor as I had known. Tracy covered up with what seemed to be a joke. He mailed the piece to me in London with a big red-crayon question mark on it. That was funny, but he actually felt hurt. I got out of it with the truth. I told him that I just didn't think of him in the same category with anyone else.

Tracy was bugged by one recurring question from the press. What advice did he have for young actors? Everyone was waiting for something profound, so he always said: "Learn your lines." He had no patience with the antics of the young actors whose school technique showed. Many times I heard him say, when a young actor or actress would demand motivation for coming in a door, "You come in the goddamn door because there's no other way to come into the goddamn room."

He had a grand acting reunion on *Guess Who's Coming to Dinner* with Katharine Hepburn. She is creative and hard-working and indefatigable. She has the genius to examine the material constantly for that little piece of something that will bring it alive or make it funnier or more poignant. But even Miss Hepburn had better not do this to Tracy too often. He could look at her until her eyes were drawn to his, almost sensing the sharp edge of his stiletto: "Why don't you just mind your own damn business, read the lines, do what he says, and let's get on with it." She'd make a funny face at him, but we got on with it.

Guess Who's Coming to Dinner was his last film. He had the energy and the verve and the desire—and not an awful lot of stamina. He was frightened for all of us that he might not get through with the picture.

Stanley Kramer directing It's a Mad, Mad, Mad, Mad World *on location on the Mojave Desert*

But he did, magnificently, as ever before. Four days before we finished, he put his arm around me and said, "You know, I read the script again last night, and if I were to die on the way home tonight you can still release the picture with what you've got."

Almost without fail, each time Spencer Tracy did an important scene, feeling the reaction of his fellow actors and the crew and the bystanders, he would call out to the cameraman, "Did you get any of it, Sam?"

Not to hear that again is a desperate thing.

Montgomery Clift in Judgment at Nuremberg

He's a very intelligent man, but like many of the Irish, his emotion is so strong that it dominates a very fine mind. By emotion, I'm including humor, a sense of the ridiculous, and everything else. This emotion means that his heart, his body, and his guts are involved.

KATHARINE HEPBURN
quoted by Jack Hamilton,
Look, July 11, 1967.

Spencer Tracy, you're the best damn actor I ever saw.

GEORGE M. COHAN
as quoted by
Damon Runyon

So Long to Spence

by DORE SCHARY

As the days grow shorter the list of dead friends whose names you have to cross out of the telephone book grows longer.

This last year, scratching out the name of Spencer Tracy was another heartbreaking wrench.

We first met thirty-seven years ago. He had made a phenomenal success on Broadway in *The Last Mile* and had gone to Hollywood to make his first film, *Up the River*. Through the kindness of Herman Shumlin, who had optioned a play of mine, I found myself playing a small role in *The Last Mile* and serving as an assistant stage manager—a job that carried a major responsibility (to me) of firing a blank shotgun cartridge into an ash can to simulate an offstage jailbreak explosion. It made a hell of a noise.

After some weeks of playing the show during the summer of 1930, I had learned (for no reason except memory exercise) the part of Killer Mears and had watched both Thomas Mitchell (who had replaced Spence) and then Allen Jenkins (who replaced Mitchell). In early fall Spence returned and slipped back into the role of Mears for a short spell. While Mitchell was all right and Jenkins excellent, Spence was simply magnificent and terrifying.

After a while we met and I gawked at him. After that we often exchanged warm intimacies such as "Good evening, Mr. Tracy" . . . "Hi, kid."

Before I left for another job I said good-bye and he bid me so long with "Good luck, Dore."

The fact that he knew my name made my day.

Two years later in Hollywood while Spence was making *Man's Castle* at Columbia Pictures, I was working there as a junior writer. I dropped in to see him on the set. I introduced myself, but he assured me he remembered. That made *that* day.

Then three years later I had an ambition realized. I was assigned by Norman Krasna to work on the film *Big City* starring Luise Rainer and Tracy.

We saw each other a few times during the making of the film—only a few. (In those days it was not *de rigeur* for writers to walk in and out of stages where their work was being filmed.) But now it was permissible for me to call him "Spence."

Shortly after the picture was released and bombed out I was for the second time fired out of MGM, but not before I had written a story and screenplay for Tracy called *Boys Town* which he had rejected. The script lay moldering on the shelf and I was finding difficulty getting a job.

Tracy then had a bad session with a bottle and while in a hospital he asked that he be put to work. He was told that the only script ready for him was *Boys Town*. He agreed to do it after a rewrite by John Meehan who shared credit with me.

The picture, directed by Norman Taurog, was ready

Dore Schary

for preview in early September. By then I was broke and preparing to pack up one child and my wife (pregnant with another child) into a well-used Ford and head back to New York with a half-finished playscript.

John Considine, the producer, invited me to the preview, which was one of those marvelous nights when everything worked out just dandy.

The picture was obviously a smash hit and I was rehired that night by Considine to work on the two Edison films which would star Mickey Rooney as Young Tom and Tracy as Edison the Man. I unpacked.

Now Spence and I got to know each other better. I was able to spend time with him. I learned of his wit and his gift for spinning anecdotes. I learned of his relationship with Pat O'Brien, Lynn Overman, Jimmy Cagney, Richard Dix, and Frank McHugh. I also learned of his most consistent insecurity syndrome: (1) his decision to do a picture; (2) then his absolute refusal to do it; (3) then his reluctant acceptance, usually a few days before the film was ready to go.

Before we ran into those three circumstances with *Edison the Man,* the Academy Awards came along and Tracy got an Oscar for his role of Father Flanagan and I got one for the original story.

After *Edison the Man,* I took on other responsibilities heading up the B-picture unit at MGM.

We would see each other often and always he had about him the aura of a star; it was there without being cultivated. Others had it, or have it—Gable, Laughton, Cooper, Cagney, Grant, Brando, Burton—others did not, or do not, even though they were or are stars. No one has defined that quality better than Ezio Pinza who said some have a motor running, others do not. (I don't know if Pinza invented the observation, but he told it to me.)

Tracy had the motor and it was always running. He worked his jaw muscle in a two shot and you forgot the other person on the screen. He listened—an actor's greatest gift. In person, he always gave you the sense of a private world in which he and no one else ever lived—he would have it no other way.

In 1943, I left MGM again. This time *I* quit. In 1948, I came back as head of production.

My first visitor was Spence.

Unannounced, he knocked on my office door. Cautiously, in answer to my "come in," he opened the door and, playing Uriah Heep, slowly shuffled toward my desk. His hands were engaged in doing a dry wash and he smiled in a simpering, fawning style. As he came toward me, he was speaking, "Excuse me, sir, for breaking in. I *do* hope you remember me. I was in your company of *Last Mile,* a long time ago."

I improvised along with him by saying I did remember him, "You're Samuel Tracy, aren't you?"

"No," he said, "Spencer—*Spencer* Tracy."

"Of course," I apologized, "I'm sorry."

"No need to, sir," he smiled. "I just wanted you to know I've never forgotten you, sir. Believe me, you can ask anyone who was in that play—I used to say—I said it all the time—you just keep your eye on that young fella—one day he's going to be head of MGM."

I couldn't go on with it. I broke up. Spence sat down. "And by Jesus," he said, "so you are, you son-of-a-bitch."

In the years that followed I discovered that Tracy, like all of us, had hardened his eccentricities.

There was a string of films: *Pat and Mike, Adam's Rib, Father of the Bride, Father's Little Dividend, Plymouth Adventure,* among others, and always he agreed to do them—cooled off—said he wouldn't do them, and finally went in front of the camera.

The last picture we did together (I was the producer) was *Bad Day at Black Rock.* At first Tracy wouldn't think of doing it. After a rewrite he said "go." On the Friday before the Monday we were to start shooting at Lone Pine in the Mojave, he strolled into the office, sat down and said, "Pappy, I got bad news. Get somebody else. I don't want to do the picture."

I had tried many ploys. Born out of desperation, a new one came to me. I said it wasn't really bad news. I was expected to turn out thirty-six films that year. If I only did thirty-five, there'd be no squawk. Tracy was relieved. Then I added, "But Spence, it may be tough for you—you see, we spent perhaps three hundred thousand on this one to date—if you don't do it, we'll have to sue you."

He gave me a long look. "You aren't kidding?"

I said, "No, I'm not."

There was another long look. Then he said, "You'll be sitting here in an air-cooled office while I'm sweating it out in Lone Pine."

"I'll go and sweat with you," I said.

"Okay," he said, "see you Monday in Black Rock."

He was there—and so was I.

In November, 1956, my career blew up at MGM (for reasons to be told at some future date). I heard from four actors: Gene Kelly, Van Johnson, Montgomery Clift—and Spence, and his summation as usual was the most lucid and most succinct....

We saw each other only a few times since that day, but occasionally in answer to a letter or a telegram he scribbled a note (he was not one for letter writing) and always I knew he was my friend.

There can be no question he was the best and most protean actor of our screen. There can also be no question he was a unique and extraordinary man.

There can also be no question that I loved him very much.

I think I'll keep his number in the book.

Tracy on Acting

I've never known what acting is. Who can honestly say what it is? A lot of people try, and they criticize actors, but I don't think they make sense. I wonder what actors are supposed to be, if not themselves. Even Laurence Olivier, the greatest of them all, just plays himself. I've finally narrowed it down to where, when I begin a part, I say to myself, this is Spencer Tracy as a judge, or this is Spencer Tracy as a priest or as a lawyer, and let it go at that. Look, the only thing an actor has to offer a director and finally an audience is his instinct. That's all.

I don't like anything about acting. But I did very well by it. I learned the trade well. It's never been very demanding. It doesn't require much brainwork. Acting is not the noblest profession in the world, but there are things lower than acting—not many, mind you—but politicians give you something to look down on from time to time.

SPENCER TRACY

SPENCER TRACY

Acid-Etched in Granite

by JAMES POWERS

There was about him, especially in the later years, something decidedly granitic. It was not only the craggy face, the jutting planes of the chin, nose, cheeks and forehead; it was something that seemed a part of the character. It worked for him as an actor, as it worked for him as a man. He was a man who inspired intimidation. In a community—Hollywood—where there seems a tendency to toady or be toadied to, where the members of the community tend to divide themselves as much by choice as assignment to the court or the courtiers, there was never any doubt where Spencer Tracy stood. Gable was The King, by someone's designation, certainly not Gable's. Humphrey Bogart in death became what he would have in life loathed most: a cult idol. These were kings too, they and Gary Cooper and John Wayne and James Stewart and—who else? Not many come to mind. And they all have something in common, about the same age.

When Spencer Tracy died, it was frequently remarked that something unique died with him. It was true. He was almost the last potent example of the great stars developed in the Golden Age of Hollywood film-making (if not of films). He was a contemporary not only of Cooper and Gable, but of Garbo, of those gilded figures whose images leaped across national barriers with the ease of air; as magnetic to alien cultures as to their own. But Tracy was not part of a period, although he came from a part of an era. He was always and relentlessly his own man, and that as much as anything is probably what made him unique.

Tracy was, first of all, in Hollywood, part of the extraordinary star system that was Metro-Goldwyn-Mayer in the 30s and 40s under the shrewd, bullying, paternalistic, wise, childish, cruel system founded and run by Louis B. Mayer. No other studio ever created and held together the stars that MGM did under Louis Mayer. Other studios, notably Warner Brothers with

its great contemporary dramas, its biographies, its musicals, may have made some better pictures, although point for point it would be a difficult argument to prove one way or the other. But even Warners, with Bette Davis, Bogart, Errol Flynn and its collection of actors and personalities, could not begin to compete with the assemblage that Mayer held in tight fief at Culver City.

Judy Garland, Elizabeth Taylor, Norma Shearer, Myrna Loy—these were contract stars at MGM. Some of them Mayer discovered and nurtured to stardom in his own peculiar fashion, a fashion that some Hollywood observers credit with the disintegration of some of these stars in their personal and professional lives after Mayer was gone and after the studio star system was gone. But if some stars were unable to face life without the protective arm of the studio, it was not so with others. Spencer Tracy survived the toppling, the crash of the great studios, and other things as well. No other star survived so long at the very top of the heap, although others did very well until death or infirmity removed them. Stewart and Wayne remain at this writing and both were somewhat younger men than Tracy.

Yet Tracy was unique and it was not alone in his staying power. Although this tenacity, of purpose and of grip on his audiences, was part of his character and his public philosophy, he was unique in other ways. Hollywood, and indeed all of what is called Show Business (Ed Wynn once remarked that he had been a member of the theatrical profession for 50 years before he knew he was in Show Biz), much of what American life is, is based on a belief that publicity is good and salubrious. Tracy didn't think so and he acted accordingly.

Tracy, almost alone of the great stars, did not have a personal press agent, even, as some do, just to keep the press off, to provide a measure of privacy. Frank

25

With Hedy Lamarr in I Take This Woman

Sinatra, for instance, whose attitude toward the press is ambivalent, although generally hostile and contemptuous, has a press agent. His job is to keep the press away, not to solicit publicity. Even in the later years, when the great studios dissolved—and with their dissolution went the vast news-gathering and news-creating and news-disseminating facilities they maintained—most stars felt compelled to employ someone of this nature if only as a convenience, so newsmen could be kept informed of their activities, personal and professional, at a minimum of interference to themselves. A press agent could take the routine telephone calls. Tracy didn't bother. And few newspapermen bothered him. It was not that they were intimidated, although Tracy had a glance that could wither or turn to stone the most impudent questioner. It was that there was nothing to ask Tracy about that he would be interested enough to answer. His private life was imperturbably his own. He was not disposed to discuss his professional life.

Tracy had a profound disregard for the American tenet, a credo heightened and refined in the theatrical world, that to be a good guy, an amiable egalitarian, is fundamental not only to show business but to American democracy. Tracy was the stoutest curmudgeon in Hollywood since W. C. Fields. He was hard-working and thoroughly professional, but he did not practice the kind of camaraderie and set-side raillery that produces so many jolly film-making experiences and so many bad pictures. Tracy never made a bad picture. Some did not succeed, but none was bad. He was a laborer, in a sense, perhaps because of his middle-class upbringing, and he gave the full value of his hire.

I do not mean to make this a eulogy. Tracy was not in some ways a likable man. He was, however, an admirable man. He could be cantankerous, even cruel with those whom he considered, even for a time, to be

dullards or dolts. In the phrase, he did not suffer fools gladly. He did not suffer them at all. On the other hand, he could be capable of great, unsolicited kindness. The operative key to this was that it was all done his own way, without any regard whatsoever for the reaction of friend or foe. This attitude, this Olympian disregard for public opinion is so rare these days as to seem eccentric. In an age when no one drops his mite into the charity hat without a tag attached, when no endowment is set up without the founder's name carved large thereon, this kind of personal, private existence, responsible only to one's own self, or to whatever philosophy the individual himself has worked out, has almost ceased to exist. It existed in Spencer Tracy.

He put himself into his work and disregarded the peripheral niceties that waste so much of so many people's time and energy. If he had a motto, it was: Let's Get On With It. This was at the core of his belief and his work. His work was for sale, but not he. People who bought his work were entitled to the best he could give, because they were paying for it, and it was an exchange, fair and traditional. But that is all they bought; his work, not him.

This was expressed in many ways, notably in his work habits. In his early days in Hollywood, he indulged in some of the roistering often associated with young men, particularly young actors. They were young gods, these men—Tracy, Gable, Montgomery, Cagney, Cooper, Taylor. They often disported themselves like the lusty Olympians so much more noted for play than the ascetic mode of the Judeo-Christian deity and his saints and prophets. There are legendary stories of drinking bouts and of pursuits of nubile girls who were then and are today coryphées to the Hollywood legend. This was youthful exuberance. It was not an essential part of Tracy. This was demonstrated in his placement of affection.

Tracy had one wife and one wife only. She is now his widow, occupied as she has been for many years with the John Tracy Clinic, a foundation which has performed notably in the field of working with deaf children, a field still needing much research. In an effort to help her own son, Mrs. Tracy founded and subsequently devoted a large part of her life to this clinic for the hearing-handicapped child. It is a delicate area to assess, that of a husband and wife, especially when each has been conspicuously reticent. But some deductions can be made.

Tracy and his wife were in a sense estranged for many years before his death. It was well known to Hollywood, and perhaps to much of the world, that there developed in these years a deep and abiding affection between Tracy and Katharine Hepburn. It tells a great deal about Tracy, and affirms some of the things we have already noted, that after the first flurry of interest in this meeting between great stars and the obvious mutual attraction that occurred, the whole affair was let very much alone. Their long and close relationship was observed by the theatrical profession and by the newsmen who make a business of covering it, yet aside from occasional remarks, offhand and disarming, nothing was made of it. After the first years of this affair, when there were the usual columnar items, each reporter hoping to be first with the bad news, it faded from public comment and public speculation. In the American tradition of plural, if tandem, marriages, Tracy and Miss Hepburn were expected to do something about it: flee to Reno or Mexico or Paris; obtain the klieg-lighted divorce; battle the pursuing press in one of those hectic contests so dear to photographers; or cooperate, as the word has it, telling all, exposing all. Then there should have followed the idyllic marriage, ripe with new promise while the happy press settled down to await the inevitable cooling and icing. It is a familiar spectacle, and the press, and one presumes, the public, seems not to mind at all if it is reprised with some of the same characters time after time. The surrender to the press, or the right of the press to the most intimate knowledge and occasion, is said to be a part of democracy. Not for Spencer Tracy or Katharine Hepburn, two sturdy Americans who knew their democracy better. They went their own way, in their own way, and what it was certainly not half a dozen people today know or are ever likely to know. Miss Hepburn, since Tracy's death, has been for the first time in her career extraordinarily available to the press. It is on her terms, to be sure, and what she talks about is what she feels at the moment like talking about. Reporters who come prepared with questions have learned it is better to switch on the tape recorder and keep mum. Miss Hepburn, like Tracy, sets the pace and directs the course. Whether they were alike in this in the beginning of their friendship is impossible to say with assurance, although it seems that they were. Perhaps this was one of the things that set off the attraction between them and kept it viable and vital. In the later years, when they played so often together, they became that rare theatrical adventure, a genuine team, not inseparable, but each somehow slightly diminished when performing with someone else.

Tracy demolishes a number of legends about Hollywood and about the theatrical profession just through the facts of his life. He was not a good fellow; he did not play that game. Yet he was eagerly sought both professionally and personally. He did not attempt to ingratiate himself with his fellow workers or the technicians in the film business. Yet he was several times nominated for an Academy Award and several times a winner. These Awards are voted by the people in motion pictures. Tracy was most rewarded, however, for the films he made early in his career, although it is in the later ones that the refinement of his style and attack is most notable and impressive. Tracy did not change greatly. It is possible to view some of the early films, *Captains Courageous, Boys Town, San Francisco,* and see in them the same Tracy of *Inherit the Wind, Judgment at Nuremberg,* and *Guess Who's Coming to Dinner.* It is not the same man or the same actor, but he can be seen there, developing, coming through.

Viewing these films, made nearly 30 years apart, several reactions occur. One is to consider how feeble is the notion that stars do not survive, that they are as unsubstantial as tinsel and as ephemeral. Untrue. The great ones do survive, and Miss Hepburn's winning of the Academy Award in 1968 demonstrated this in a manner unlikely to be duplicated. It was her second Award. Her first had been 35 years earlier. Another is to observe how Tracy had aged and learned. The two, of course, are not necessarily synonymous. It is possible to see actors of almost exactly the same age and career range as Tracy and observe what different things can occur. Some actors may age gracefully and be a different kind of actor at 50 than at 25. Others age uncomfortably, seeming to stretch the loosening skinbag tightly in boyish capers. Tracy was quintessential. What he was doing the last year of his life, in *Guess Who's Coming to Dinner,* was what he was doing in *Boom Town.* He had simply learned how to do it better.

Art, it is sometimes said, is economical; less is better. This, like most becoming brevities, is not quite the whole story. Not always. But sometimes it is true. And it was true with Tracy.

With Katharine Hepburn in Woman of the Year

If it is so that an actor's most essential quality is conviction—and surely it is, because all else must rest on that; if we are not convinced the actor is who he represents himself to be for that speech, that act, that movie, he has surely lost us—then we see the heart of Tracy's great gift. He was because he willed himself to be. Whether intuitive or learned, his greatest skill was that we believed him because he convinced us we should. It is the despair of critics to isolate this factor and justify it. Read Shaw, read Hazlitt, read any of the worthy modern critics, Stark Young to James Agee. They all, we all, stumble on this one fact. One can go into character delineation, into line reading, into body movement, and yet that is all exploration after the fact. It is significant that a line most often attributed to Spencer Tracy wasn't even said by him at all. It had to do with rules for acting. "Learn your lines and don't bump into the furniture," Tracy is supposed to have said. Alfred Lunt said it, and he is quite another kind of actor. Lunt didn't mean it, and Tracy might have—at the moment—although Tracy did not think what he did and others tried to do was easy. So it is even less easy to evaluate, or to render in terms from one medium of expression to another.

An actor like Olivier is a joy for critics. He is always getting done up in some makeup that is impossible to ignore. He works at an accent. He works at expanding the range or volume of his voice. He plays widely disparate characters. There is something for a critic to get hold of. Comparing *The Entertainer* with *Othello* is good for thousands of words in itself. Tracy didn't do that. The only time he went at all outside himself was in *Captains Courageous*. There, and perhaps in *The Old Man and the Sea,* he attempted a poetic quality that was at variance with the roles he customarily played. He was content to try, but in summary evaluation these seem to have been the least successful of his characterizations.

But it does no good to say, and by saying, dismiss the man, that Tracy always played himself. Of course he did. He was that kind of actor. He was not playing the man Tracy as we might have known him, if we could have known him personally. That is nonsense. He was playing in the style of Tracy the actor as he had come to know it, use it, make it work, refine it, over the years. In that sense, he always played himself. But to use this as a basis for derogatory criticism is as footling as chiding Whistler because he did not paint in the style of Augustus Johns. Even with Olivier we do not say he is Hamlet. We say and know he is playing Hamlet, and we know there will be others who will play Hamlet and they will be very different. If we like Olivier as Hamlet then it is Olivier's Hamlet that we like, it is the essential quality Olivier has brought to the role that only he has. The vocal pyro-

With Fredric March in Inherit the Wind

technics, the other studies made of the character and of the play, are only embroideries. It is, as they say in Show Business, Olivier that we buy.

Tracy was not a great actor in the way that Olivier has been. He did not have the range, or if he did have it, did not explore it. He found a manner of making a living that with all its foolishness he enjoyed, and that rewarded him in a manner he considered proper. He was at all times a professional—he knew his lines, he was on time and expected others to be, and he did not make allowances for the amateurism or gaucheries of others. Quitting time was quitting time, and Tracy did not work beyond it. There was a story legendary in Hollywood for years about that. In the early days, movies were made seven days a week and then six days, and finally, when the unions achieved some power, five days a week. Work hours were long, and still are, but actors these days are paid overtime, supper penalty, and other benefits if the director or producer has not properly organized himself so the shooting schedule fits within the normal hours. Tracy established his own working hours early in his career. His working day ended at five, although six, seven, and on into the morning is not unusual for some movie-filming. It is said that one day, a few minutes before five, a scene ended. The director, new to Tracy, began an explanation of what the next scene would be. "Now," he said, or so the story goes, "in this next scene we will all assemble on Stage Nine." "You will. I won't," responded Tracy, as he tucked in his gear and went home. But while he was there he worked and he expected others to do the same.

If Tracy did not have a wide range, if perhaps he determined early that his range was a limited one, then it was a wise decision, and within that range Tracy was incomparable. Like most of the great stars of his career range, Tracy had early stage training. He and Clark Gable, for instance, were both taken for motion pictures because of the same play, *The Last Mile,* which both played, Tracy in New York and Gable in Los Angeles. Yet unlike many other stars of stage background, Tracy never expressed any desire to return to the stage. He was not one of those who yearned for the so-called real theater. There is no doubt he could have been a most successful stage actor. His self-possession, his confidence—above all, his abiding conviction—would have been as effective onstage as they were on film. But he did not care to do it and he never did.

It was widely known in Hollywood, as somehow those things are, that Spencer Tracy was dying while he was making *Guess Who's Coming to Dinner.* Stanley Kramer, the producer-director of that film, had been one of Tracy's few friends, and a man with whom he worked more often than with any other director or producer. It was a curious combination. Tracy, generally glum and taciturn; Kramer, usually cheerful and inclined to verbalize. It probably worked as well as it did, this combination, because Kramer is the kind of director he is, not because or in spite of the kind of man he is. Kramer is not a heavy director. He does not have rigid notions of how a scene or a character should be played. He has made sure consistently in his films to get very good actors, and he very often then gives them their head. He was for a time a film editor, and he knows what can be done with film, a facet of movies that a great many directors—some of them very successful—are not familiar with. At any rate, Kramer greatly admired Tracy and there is some belief that he would have gone ahead and made *Guess Who's Coming to Dinner* even if he had known Tracy would die in the middle of it. Kramer's admirations are few but they are strong.

If Tracy knew he was in the midst of his last days, he gave no indication during the filming of the picture. It has become popular now to say, in a particularly nasty kind of comment, that Tracy was nominated for an Academy Award for that picture because he was

With Katharine Hepburn in Woman of the Year

dying. This sort of remark displays an ignorance of Hollywood. The nomination may have been awry; Tracy may have given better performances that did not get nominated, but the nomination was deserved. The members of the Academy occasionally assess work as a body, and then a nomination may be made that seems to lack logic, but it has its own special meaning.

Tracy worked as hard on this last film as he did on any of his films, which means with close attention to all details, to scenes he was not in, to actors he would never work with. He was concerned with the total picture, because it all reflected on him. If he could be aloof, as he usually was, not out of disdain, but as a part of securing his own person, not scattering it to the winds through unnecessary and meaningless badinage, he could also act with conspicuous gallantry. There was an incident on the filming of *Judgment at Nuremberg,* during one scene in which Tracy was not involved, where he spotted an actress playing a very small role. She had been starred with him in a film 16 or 18 years before and now, in the way those things sometimes went, she was playing smaller roles. There was nothing maudlin about it. She was professional, as was he. But Tracy could feel how this might affect a woman, if not an actress. When the scene broke, he gathered himself up out of his canvas chair, stencilled with his name on the back, as were the few such chairs reserved for the director and stars. He walked across the big set, the reproduction of the courtroom at Nuremberg. He spoke to the actress, reminded her of their past association, which, of course, she remembered very, very well, and had wondered if he had, if she might have approached him. Tracy chatted, begged off courteously, and returned to his chair.

To one who does not know Hollywood, the scene itself is difficult to recreate. There is an aura on a set, especially one of a major film, where seconds tick in terms of thousands of dollars. There is an increased atmosphere when there are on the set the major stars, such as Spencer Tracy. They are in the corner of everyone's eyes. They cannot make a movement that is not caught, evaluated, judged. Tracy, while he was unpretentious, was not unaware of his power. He knew he had only to indicate and his whim would be honored. He knew that from that moment forward, the actress' life on that picture would be a little easier; assistant directors, not just sure of what position she held, would be deferential; a chair of some sort might be found for her, her contract might be expanded by a few days. He could have done it differently, of course. He could have called attention to himself and to her and achieved all the same things.

But that was not Spencer Tracy's style. His style was a quiet one, but most effective.

A Tracy Interview

"The last few pictures I've tried, God knows I've failed," he said. "You know what happened to *The Old Man and the Sea*. And a critic or two took care of *Inherit the Wind.*" The subject of audiences came up. "Young people today want the thrill of a *Psycho,* for the love of God," Tracy said. "I don't get to the young people. What the hell do they want to see me for? They don't go to see an old man. The older people go because they think they *might* see something good."

"Olivier is the best actor today," he went on. When I see him, I'm never in doubt that it's Larry. When someone sees me, he knows it's Tracy. I'm not trying to become someone else. I watch David Susskind looking down his nose, talking about what acting is. I can't explain what it is. I had a wonderful teacher in George M. Cohan, and he couldn't explain it. My three years with George M., they were the most important. Cohan said to me: 'Spencer, you have to act less.'

"I don't know how anyone makes money on a movie today," he said suddenly. "Costs are up so much. So there's greater tension on the set. Hollywood is dying because it costs too much to make a movie.

"You know what the trouble with the industry is? In the old days, if you wanted to see Laurette Taylor you went to the theater and paid $4. Now actors are refereeing football games and opening drugstores. You know, they are stupid. Originally we were like a closed circus. Remember how tough a circus used to be to sneak into? Personal appearances are a lot of hooey."

Does Tracy feel that he has changed over the years? "I've become grouchier," he said. "The 30 years have gone by awfully fast. My rewards have been doing things like *The Old Man and the Sea,* though it was a flop—my days at Metro—*Captains Courageous,* which was my best role."

What could he teach young actors? "I'd tell them to throw their gum away and to keep cigarettes out of their mugs. But I couldn't teach them, because I don't know anything about acting."

from an interview by Jack Nugent, *Newsweek,* January 9, 1961.

Young Spencer Tracy

Biography

Spencer Bonaventure Tracy was born in Milwaukee, Wisconsin, on April 5, 1900, the son of John Edward and Caroline Brown Tracy. Carroll, his brother, had been born four years earlier in Freeport, Illinois. At the time of Spencer's birth, the family lived on Prospect Avenue in the Tory Hill district of Milwaukee. John Tracy was general sales manager of the Sterling Motor Truck Company.

Spencer Tracy later wrote:

My mother tells me that we lived on "the right side of the tracks," though that probably didn't make much difference to my dad, who was Irish with generations of good old Irish fighters behind him. My mother gives the family its old American colonial stock. Her lineage goes directly back to settlers in the colonies before the Revolution.

Maybe it was the Irish blood in me that gave me the itch to wander away. I can't say that I ever loved school, though I did finally struggle through the second year of college. We lived in a pleasant environment in Milwaukee, yet they tell me that when I was seven years old I ran away. That was the beginning of the wanderlust, I suppose. They found me a little after dark. I was down on the south side playing in an alley with two youngsters known in the neighborhood as Mousie and Rattle. They were sons of a bartender, tough eggs, I suppose, but we became darned good friends. The question of how I happened to bump into them has never been settled. I remember how my mother grabbed me and wept when I got back home. That should have cured me of running away, but it didn't.

I have no particularly joyful recollection of school, grammar school, at any rate. For some reason I just couldn't get interested in books. They bored me. I tried spasmodically to be interested. I managed to stagger along from grade to grade, just getting by on passing marks and an occasional ability to kid the teachers along. I did get a kick out of athletics at the various grammar schools that admitted me, and eventually I won a diploma from Saint Rosa's parochial school. Boy, that was a gala day.

When he was sixteen, the Tracy family moved to Kansas City, the father's business taking them there. Spencer attended two schools there; but in about six months the family moved back to Milwaukee. Spencer wanted to quit school and go to work, but his father insisted he finish his education. So Spencer enrolled at Marquette Academy. There he met William J. O'Brien, later to be known as Pat O'Brien.

On April 6, 1917, the United States entered World War I. There suddenly were flags in the streets. Men in uniform were marching past the school at all hours of the day. Bands played stirring marches and patriotic slogans were written on the school blackboards.

Apart from the fact that I'd never passed up many fights, this war didn't appeal to me so much as a fight, but as a chance to go places and see things. Maybe some of the hysteria and patriotic ballyhoo did get under my skin, because after all, I was seventeen years old and those things appeal to kid minds. But, most of all, it was a chance to get out of school once and for all, pack up and get right smack into the middle of a lot of excitement.

One winter afternoon after school, Spencer jumped on a streetcar and rode downtown. Near Milwaukee's famous Schlitz Hotel was the Marine Recruiting Office. Spencer hesitated and then went in, and told the gentleman at the desk he wanted to enlist. The officer asked a number of questions, taking down the information, until he got to the question of age. Spencer had planned to say he was twenty, but instead he stammered out the truth that he was only seventeen. The officer told him he was too young to enlist. Tracy went home disappointed.

In the meantime, Pat O'Brien had joined the Navy. When Spencer explained what had happened, O'Brien told him the Navy didn't require the applicant's age for enlistment. So the next day Tracy joined the Navy, and surprised his parents with the news. Both Tracy and O'Brien were sent to the Great Lakes Naval Training Center for their basic training. Six months later Tracy was sent to the Norfolk Navy Yard in Virginia, and was still there when the war ended.

Tracy was discharged and returned to Milwaukee. The government offered a thirty-dollar-a-month pension for any serviceman who wanted to continue his

Spencer Tracy at the age of twelve in Milwaukee, Wisconsin

schooling. Since he had no specific plans, Spencer returned to Marquette, and then transferred to Northwestern Military Academy at Lake Geneva, Wisconsin. John Tracy hoped that his son might come to work for nim in the trucking business when he finished high school, but Spencer decided to go to college.

In 1921, Spencer Tracy enrolled at Ripon College as a pre-med student. He thought he might become a plastic surgeon. One of his teachers, Professor H. P. Boody, suggested he join the debating team. Spencer did, found himself gaining self-confidence, and soon discovered he enjoyed debating anyone on any subject.

To my vast surprise, I liked it. It helped me develop memory for lines that has been a godsend since I started stage work; it gave me something of a stage presence; and it helped get rid of my awkwardness. Also, I gradually developed the ability to speak extemporaneously, which has stood me in good stead many a time when a cue has been missed.

In March of 1921, Professor J. Clark Graham was casting the commencement play, which would be Clyde Fitch's *The Truth*. Professor Graham later wrote:

One evening, a student who had acted in several plays that I had directed called up. "There is a fellow in our house who is interested in acting," he said. "I believe he has real talent. He would like to try out for our next play. Could I bring him over?"

They arrived in a few minutes. Tracy was a fine looking lad, more mature in appearance than the average freshman. I noted especially a certain decisiveness in his speech, a clipped firmness of expression indicating poise, self-control, and confidence. I was impressed and invited him to try out for our next play. He won the leading role and gave an excellent performance.

The campus newspaper, *College Days,* reported the following: "Mr. Tracy proved himself a consistent and unusually strong actor in this most difficult straight part. His steadiness, his reserve strength and suppressed emotion were a pleasant surprise to all who heard him as the Warder."

Professor Graham recalled:

The following fall he took the lead in a one-act play as a heroic prisoner. I think the play was *The Valiant.* Before the end of the semester he was talking about a career as an actor. His parents came on a visit and we had a family conference. As a result I wrote Mr. Sargent of the American Academy of Dramatic Arts in New York and he suggested that Tracy appear for a tryout.

While traveling with the debating team as it toured several East Coast colleges, Tracy stopped at the Sargent school in New York City. He auditioned, using his role from *The Valiant,* and was accepted. Spencer's father was not enthusiastic. "It sounds like a silly idea to me, but if you have your mind set on it, I'll go halfway with you." John agreed to pay the tuition for the first semester if Spencer would live on the thirty dollars a month from the government.

In New York City, Tracy again met O'Brien, who was also studying acting at Sargent's school. They pooled their limited resources and took a room in a lodging house.

Pat O'Brien later wrote in his autobiography:

Entering Sargent's school was all I wanted at the moment. Spencer and I rented a mouse-nest of a room at Ninety-eighth and West End Avenue. It was two steep, shady flights up, but as Spencer said, "It has a ceiling." Our landlady, Mrs. Brown, admired actors and treated us like established stars. But pretzels and water was a frequent diet for Tracy and O'Brien, and I learned to wear my socks from either end.

I discovered that beyond the glittering theater world of lights and color and success, there was another, a larger world of struggling actors, students, and would-be actors. The unknown people of the night, an underworld of yet submerged talent existed, looking for the break, the opening, the chance.

Like Spencer and myself, mostly they lived in odd corners of the city near the theaters, in dank little rooms lit by gas, or one flickering light bulb. Waiting meanly, trying to keep their few clothes neat and brushed, moving about on the fringe of the theater world; full believers in miracles. We were frozen in winter when the gray wind came up Broadway from the direction of Macy's. In summer, in our mean rooms under slate roofs the heat was out of Egypt. But somehow we didn't really mind. Actually we were often very happy. Discomfort and poverty are not the evils our over-socially-progressed age has pictured them. Lack of hope is the true horror.

And Spencer also remembered those days.

That thirty dollars a month, though, didn't go as

Spencer Tracy (third from left) as a robot in R.U.R.

University of Texas

35

far as I thought it would. Invariably I was broke several days before the end of each month. Sometimes I could borrow a couple of dollars from Pat, and sometimes he was broke ahead of me.

I studied dramatics as I'd never studied anything before in my life. Always in the back of my mind was the idea that I'd never have enough money to finish the course, and that I'd better learn all I could as fast as I could. Pat and I used to read lines to each other, rearrange the furniture, and pace back and forth doing bits of business as if we were in front of the footlights, until some other roomer shouted to us to shut up so that he could go to sleep.

To look back on it now, it was lots of fun—all but tightening up our belts the last few days of every month. There's something about going hungry that makes you discover the utmost of your resources.

The debts mounted. Tracy realized that he had to get a job or return home defeated. For three days, he went from agent to agent, from theater to theater, and then, on the afternoon of the third day, when his hopes had sunk very low, he got a job. The Theatre Guild was preparing Karel Capek's science-fantasy *R.U.R.* (Rossum's Universal Robots) for its American premiere at the Garrick Theatre. Tracy got a nonspeak-ing part as one of the robots. His salary was fifteen dollars a week. O'Brien was also employed as one of the robots. The show opened on October 9, 1932. During the run, Tracy got a small speaking part and a raise in salary. In November, the play was moved to the Frazee Theater where it continued its run into the early spring of 1923, closing after 184 performances.

Out of work, Tracy heard about a new stock company that Leonard Wood, Jr., had formed in White Plains, New York. Tracy contacted the manager, was hired at a salary of twenty dollars a week, and joined the company for its second production. Louise Treadwell, an actress in the same company, was returning from a week-end in New York City. To the front of the coach she noticed a young man. When both of them got off the train at White Plains, he spoke to her, and they discovered that they both were working for the Leonard Wood company. In *The Man Who Came Back,* his first play for the company, Spencer played two character parts. Then he played other roles in subsequent productions. Some weeks later the company moved to the Empire Theater in Fall River, Massachusetts. There, on June 11, 1923, Tracy played the part of Algy Riggs in the company's production of *Getting Gertie's Garter.* The next week, June 18, he played the part of the detective in *Lawful Larceny.* The company produced three more plays in which Spencer Tracy did not appear, closing its run in July.

On September 10, 1923, the Stuart Walker Company, a stock company in Cincinnati, Ohio, opened a play called *The Gypsy Trail,* in which Spencer played the role of Stiles.

Two days later, on the twelfth of September, 1923, Spencer Tracy and Louise Treadwell were married in Cincinnati.

Two weeks later, Spencer played the role of George Crooper in the Walker Company production of Booth Tarkington's play *Seventeen.* The Stuart Walker Company performed twenty-eight plays during a season of twenty-eight weeks. The company consisted of sixty-seven players, twenty-four of whom were listed as leads, and thirty of whom had performed previously on Broadway. Members of this company included Blanche Yurka, Tom Springer, William Kirkland, Albert Hackett, and Spring Byington.

A new comedy, *A Royal Fandango,* by Zoe Atkins was slated for Broadway, with Jose Allesandro, a newly discovered star from Argentina, appearing opposite Ethel Barrymore. Spencer obtained a part. The play tried out in Washington, D.C., and then opened in New York City on November 12, 1923. "Ridiculous, utterly impossible, far-fetched" were the adjectives used by the critics to describe the play. It closed after twenty-four performances.

Some years later Mr. Tracy said: "My ego took an

THE WOOD PLAYERS
IN
"The Man Who Came Back"

A Drama in Five Episodes by Jules Eckert Goodman
Staged and Directed by the Belasco of Stock
KENDAL WESTON

(The characters as you meet them)

Griggs, a Butler...Thomas Williams
Mrs. Gaynes, Thomas Potter's sister.........................Alma Powell
Thomas Potter, Banker and Broker.........................Chas. S. Greene
Charles Reisling, his "Man Friday"..........................Fairfax Burgher
Henry Potter, Potter's only child.............................Ernest Woodward
Daisy Maitland, of the Cabarets............................Dolores Graves
Flossie Columbia, another......................................Helene Niles
Willie Simpson, a young spender...........................Edward Crandall
Archie Dunton, a boon companion...........................Thomas Hudson
Olive...Helen Edwards
Captain Trevalan...Valentine Winter
Captain Gallon..Spencer Tracy
Marcelle...Louise Treadwell
Gibson, Manager of the Cabaret...........................Frederick Hargrave
Binksie, a dope..Spencer Tracy
Sam Shew Sing, Keeper of the Den........................Frederick Hargrave
Flossie, from Frisco..Dolores Graves
Nellie, a dope..Helene Niles

Boys, Girls, Sailors, Etc.

SYNOPSIS OF SCENES

FIRST EPISODE—Breakfast room in the home of Thomas Potter, New York City. "The distance between New York and San Francisco is 3,170 miles."

SECOND EPISODE—"The Breakers" Cafe in San Francisco, California. Six months later. "The distance from San Francisco to Shanghai, China, is 6,500 miles."

THIRD EPISODE—Sam Shew's Opium Joint, near Shanghai, China. Six months later. "The distance between Shanghai and Honolulu is 4,360 miles."

FOURTH EPISODE—Henry Potter's Pinery, near Honolulu, one year later. "The distance from Honolulu to New York is 5,370 miles."

FIFTH EPISODE—Same as first episode. Seven months later.

Stage Manager—CHAS. S. BARTON
Scenery painted by Fisher.

awful beating, though, when I read the notices the day after we opened. One caustic critic commented that I looked as if I had been picked up by the property man. I can laugh about that now but did it burn me up at the time!" Actually the critic made the statement not only about Mr. Tracy, but about the entire supporting cast, which included Charles Eaton, Beverly Silgraves, and Edward G. Robinson.

For the remainder of the year, Spencer took a job with a stock company in Elizabeth, New Jersey. Then, in January, 1924, both Mr. and Mrs. Tracy performed for a stock company in Winnepeg, Canada. As always, Spencer went first to be certain of a contract. But after a few weeks the company had to close its doors. The manager called the Tracys into his office, and expressed his appreciation of their work. Then he offered to pay their return fare, something unsuccessful companies seldom did.

In April, Spencer worked for the W. H. Wright Company in Pittsburgh, Pennsylvania. Throughout the 1920s, William Wright organized several stock companies in various cities and under various names. The concept of stock companies today is somewhat different from the stock companies of an earlier period, which performed at least one new play each week. As Pat O'Brien recalled in his book:

> In those days actors playing in stock companies were doing four things simultaneously. They were *playing* the play, *forgetting* a play, *studying* a play, and *rehearsing* a play. All because each week we did a different production, and in many of the companies around the nation, they did two plays a week. It was hard, brain-tormenting, bone-breaking work, but gratifying.

By June of that year, William Wright had moved his stock company to Grand Rapids, Michigan. Spencer went with him. Mrs. Tracy stayed in Milwaukee with his parents, and on June 26, 1924, a son was born to Louise and Spencer. They named him John.

The Wright Company occasionally tested plays for Broadway. One such play was called *Page the Duke*. New York manager Earle Booth came to see the play. He didn't like it, but he was enthusiastic about Spencer's performance. The play closed. Later Mr. Booth offered Spencer a contract for another play, *The Sheepman*, which was being tried out on the East Coast. Tracy took the job, but the play closed before it reached Broadway.

During October, Spencer began a winter season at the Montauk Theater in Brooklyn, New York. It was at this time that the Tracys discovered their son's deafness. When Spencer completed his Brooklyn engage-

ment in the spring of 1925, he returned to Grand Rapids to work with Mr. Wright's company at the Power's Theater in the late spring and early summer.

Late in 1925, Spencer Tracy joined the Trent Theater Stock Company in Trenton, New Jersey, for their winter season. He appeared in every production, usually as the lead.

Some years later, when the Trent Theater was torn down, an article which appeared in the *Trenton Times* contained the following paragraph:

> Certainly among all of those who have appeared on the Trent stage in stock the one who is best known to millions of motion picture patrons is Spencer Tracy, who received his apprenticeship as an actor in that hard school of "a play a week" as shown behind the footlights in the days when repertory companies flourished.

Besides nightly performances (with one night off a week) the Trent company usually also presented four matinees a week.

The season opened on November 3, 1925, with Mr. Tracy starring opposite Ethel Remey and Louise Huntington in *The Best People*. The second play (beginning

Program page for A Royal Fandango, *1923*

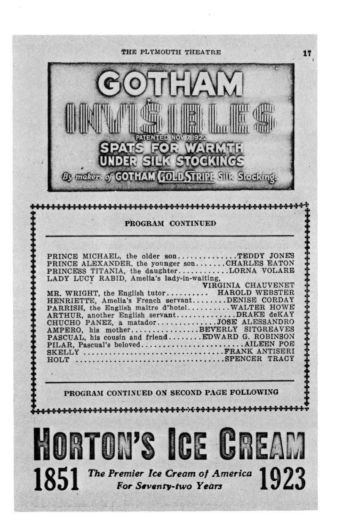

Spencer Tracy with his mother, Mrs. Carrie B. Tracy, and his brother Carroll Tracy

November 9) was George M. Cohan's *The Song and Dance Man.*

A review commenting on the play made the following remarks, which could be applied to the career of any actor:

> Have you ever gone to a show and wondered just what were the real offstage personalities of the various players you have seen? Did it ever occur to you that they are just human beings, like yourself, with all the petty likes and dislikes, good points and bad, that you encounter in everyone in the world?
>
> The personality of a player, once the grease paint is removed and he is "all washed up," to use a trade expression, is vastly different, once out of the limelight.
>
> The actor has his hopes and fears, his ups and downs, his joys and sorrows, just as do all of us. And furthermore, the actor is thoroughly human. If he wasn't human to the core, he couldn't be a successful actor; in fact, he couldn't be an actor at all.

The *Trenton Times* of November 10 said: "Spencer Tracy assumed the title role—the same role that Mr. Cohan himself had in his original company. And Mr. Tracy was true to his part, acting with an exactness that several times brought him rounds of applause from a fair-sized first-night audience."

On November 12, the paper reported the following: "Mr. Tracy is being enthusiastically received at every performance. The part of the song and dance man is one of the most difficult to handle and required an unusually large amount of study. It is a long role and many of the speeches in it are the longest ever written for a part."

On December 8, 1925, in a review of the next play, *The Back Slapper,* the *Evening Times* said: "Spencer

Tracy and Ethel Remey have the leading parts, as usual, and it so hurt us to see Mr. Tracy, ordinarily such a gentlemanly personage, trying to enact the part of a villain, a tyrannical husband, in the second and last acts."

The same newspaper reviewed the next play on December 22. "Langdon McCormick came to the Trent Theater last night with his latest stage success, *Shipwrecked,* and took a good-sized Monday night audience through one of the most sensational and thrilling melodramas they have ever witnessed by the Trent Stock Company. For the play, which seems to border on the impossible when it comes to scenic effects, is replete with thrills; tense moments and witty lines are thrown in here and there, giving the necessary humorous touch.

"Needless to say, *Shipwrecked* far exceeds anything shown at the Trent this season, and rightly it should. The cost in producing it for the people of Trenton exceeds over $2,000 the cost of the average play presented by Frank McCoy and his players. Spencer Tracy comes into his own this week with a real part and takes it to perfection, playing, of course, opposite Ethel Remey."

"*Buddies,* George Hobart's song play will be the offering at the Trent next week, beginning Monday matinee," announced the Trenton *Evening Times* on December 26. "There will be several added performances next week, a matinee every day and a special holiday midnight show on New Year's Eve, starting at 11:30 o'clock.

"And several added attractions will mark the presentation of *Buddies.* There will be a jazz band orchestral accompaniment for the song and dance numbers in which the favorites of the company will appear. Mildred McLeod, a Broadway star, will join the cast, and appear with Harry Clarke in a series of clever numbers. Ethel Remey and Spencer Tracy will have the leading roles of the piece."

The play was reviewed on December 29. "Spencer Tracy, as the tongue-tied bashful 'Babe' had the audience with him from the very start, and when he finally managed to, by accident, gasp out a proposal to the girl he loved, they hung on his words with the breathless anticipation of a poor relative."

The first week of January, 1926, Mr. Tracy and Miss Remey played the leads in a farce, *Wedding Bells,* which the critic said seemed to be written for them.

On January 12, there appeared this note about Frank McCoy's next production, *Quincy Adams Sawyer.* "To make the play more realistic a real, old-fashioned husking bee is held in the third act, and the players seem to take real enjoyment in doing an honest-to-goodness Virginia Reel. During the bee Tracy finds the red ear of corn and is penalized by having to kiss every girl present."

The final play of the season at the Trent was *The*

Spencer Tracy with his children Susie and John

Family Upstairs. The January 22 review said: "In the leading roles Miss Remey and Spencer Tracy are receiving a warm reception, due to the fact that the parts fit their respective talents to the point of perfection."

For the late spring and summer season, Spencer Tracy returned to Grand Rapids to again appear with the Wright Company. In August he received a letter from Selena Royle, an actress he had worked with in stock. She was in New York City and had obtained a part in a new play, *Yellow,* being produced by George M. Cohan. A role in the play had not yet been filled and she was recommending Tracy for it. Spencer immediately went to New York and auditioned for the part. Cohan hired him. The three-act melodrama opened at the National Theater on September 21, 1926. In the cast were Chester Morris, Selena Royle, Hale Hamilton, Marjorie Wood, Shirley Warde, and Spencer Tracy. The play ran for 135 performances, although it received mixed reviews. Sometime later the following item appeared in a New York newspaper:

In September 1926 George M. Cohan produced a play called *Yellow* by Margaret Vernon. Rehearsals did not go smoothly, and Cohan fussed and fumed over every member of the cast—except one young man in a relatively minor role. The young man took Cohan's apparent lack of interest as a sure sign that he was doomed to dismissal, and though he played every run-through as well as he could, he expected to get the sack at any moment. When the dress rehearsal was finished, however, Cohan spoke to him for the first time. In front of the entire company he said, "Spencer Tracy, you're the best damn actor I ever saw," and walked out of the theater.

It was signed Damon Runyon. Cohan was not a man given to praising other actors. Spencer took the newspaper clipping home and proudly showed it to Louise. During the run of the play, Cohan told Tracy that he was writing a part for him in a new play. *Yellow* closed in January, 1927. Spencer then played in the road company of the Theatre Guild's production of *Ned McCobb's Daughter* for eight weeks, part of that time in Chicago.

On April 12, 1927, The Lima (Ohio) *News* announced the opening of a new stock company. "The Wright Players, who will open the stock season at the Faurot [Theater] next Sunday, arrived in Lima Monday and immediately started rehersals for their opening day, of *Laff That Off* a sparkling comedy-drama which has just closed its successful run on Broadway. . . .

"Heading the cast are Miss Louise Treadwell and Spencer Tracy, both of whom have had unlimited experience both in stock and musical comedy field."

Because of illness Louise Treadwell did not appear in the first production, but beginning with the second play, *The Patsy,* she played the lead opposite Spencer in the next nine productions. From the middle of April until the end of June, the Wright Players presented a new play each week. The plays were *The First Year, Smilin' Through, The Family Upstairs, The Best People, The Cat and the Canary, The Alarm Clock, Apple-*

With daughter Susie

sauce, and *The Whole Town's Talking.*

Harry Horne was director of the Wright Players for the summer season at the Faurot Theater.

His [Horne's] job in Lima isn't so difficult, he says, because of the high standards of the cast, their ability to grasp things quickly and remember them, the conscientious manner in which they go at their work and the finished manner in which they present it.

For instance, the average person can hardly imagine so fine a Sunday afternoon performance as the Wright Players have already given on three occasions without loads of rehearsals. And yet, all told, these players have but five opportunities to rehearse a production. Monday at 10 A.M. the company meets and each player is assigned to his or her part, with Horne elucidating as they go along. The play is read through with the stage instructions indicated at the same time. This differs from the old-time method in which the parts are given out to be memorized before the company is called together for rehearsal.

The Lima *News* reported the following on June 26, 1927. "Announcement of the resignation of Louise Treadwell and Spencer Tracy as leading members of the Wright Players has been made by H. F. Bodie, manager of the company. Tracy and his wife will leave soon for New York City where the former will start rehearsals for *Cyclone,* a new George M. Cohan play."

Returning to New York City, Tracy soon began work on the role Mr. Cohan had especially written for him. The farce, *The Baby Cyclone,* revolved around a pet Pekinese, over which two couples were constantly quarreling. Mr. Tracy played one of the husbands. Others in the cast were Joseph Holickey, Agnes Gilda, Nan Sunderland, Grant Mitchell, John Boyle, and Natalie Moorehead. The play opened on September 12, 1927, at the Henry Miller Theater and ran for 184 performances. After the play closed in the spring of 1928, Tracy joined the road company of another Cohan hit, *Whispering Friends,* taking over the role originated by William Harrigan.

1929 was the year of the St. Valentine's Day massacre; gangster killings in Chicago; the Kellogg-Briand Treaty, in which sixty-two world powers renounced war; the conviction of Albert Fall, former Secretary of the Interior, for accepting a bribe in connection with the leasing of the Teapot Dome oil reserve; and the stock market crash which marked the end of the post-

National Theatre
41st Street, West of Broadway
'Phone Pennsylvania 0808
WALTER C. JORDAN and SAM S. and LEE SHUBERT, INC., Lessees
Direction of LEE and J. J. SHUBERT

FIRE NOTICE: Look around NOW and choose the nearest Exit to your seat. In case of fire, walk (not run) to THAT Exit. Do not try to beat your neighbor to the street.
JOHN J. DORMAN, Fire Commissioner.

BEGINNING TUESDAY NIGHT, SEPTEMBER 21, 1926
Matinees Wednesday and Saturday

A NEW AMERICAN MELODRAMA
"YELLOW"
In 8 Scenes
By MARGARET VERNON
Under the Management of George M. Cohan
Staged by John Meehan—Sets by Joseph Wickes Studio

The Cast

HOTEL PORTER, at N. Y. Hotel	JOSEPH GUTHRIE
"VAL" PARKER, a Young Architect	CHESTER MORRIS
HOTEL WAITER, at N. Y. Hotel	JOSE RIVAS
"POLLY," Daughter of T. W. Sayre	SELENA ROYLE
JACK CROMPTON, a New York Business Man	HALE HAMILTON
JEN WILKES, Jim's Wife	MARJORIE WOOD
DAISY LINGARD, the Hide-away Girl	SHIRLEY WARDE
JIMMY WILKES, a Bank Clerk	SPENCER TRACY
THOMAS W. SAYRE, a Retired Merchant	FRANK KINGDON
MRS. SAYRE, His Wife	JANE WHEATLEY
PAUL, Crompton's Man Servant	RICHARD FREEMAN
DONALDSON, a Plainclothes Man	DANIEL PENNELL
CARRIE WILLIAMS, a Colored Maid	EVA CASSANOVA
WELLES, a Copper	MARTIN MALLOY
INSPECTOR GRANEY, at the Helm	HARRY C. BANNISTER
LOUIS, a Restaurant Manager	H. PAUL DOUCET
CIGARET GIRL	MARY MEEHAN
PAGE BOY	LEE CHANNER
CHECK GIRL	HELEN MACKS
AN OLD ROUE	FRANK BURBECK
JOHNSON, a Starter	FREDERICK SMITH
POLICEMAN	PAUL HANSON

PROGRAM CONTINUED ON NEXT PAGE

New York Public Library

war prosperity. That year Spencer Tracy appeared in four failures.

On March 6, a new play by Warren Lawrence entitled *Conflict* opened at the Fulton Theatre. Tracy played the role of Richard Banks, a clerk who returns from the First World War a decorated flyer. He marries his former employer's niece, finds the marriage cannot work due to social differences, divorces her and goes into commercial aviation. The play was staged by Edward Clarke Lilley, and the cast included Edward Arnold, George Meeker, Peggy Allenby, and Albert Dekker. It closed after thirty-seven performances.

"*Conflict* came to the Fulton Theatre with very little heralding and departed so soon after its premiere that one hesitates to say anything about it except by way of recording its appearance," wrote *Theatre* magazine, May, 1929. "Warren F. Lawrence, its author, has written some vital and moving scenes, and in the person of Spencer Tracy he had a standard bearer of great excellence. In point of fact, the whole action revolved around the character of 'Richard Banks,' whose evolu-

tion from a drab and ineffectual clerk to flight commander of the 361st Aero Squadron is one of the notable performances of the season, and Mr. Tracy is that 'Richard Banks,' an ace whose skill and daring in bringing down the enemy's planes makes him famous and results in his undoing. The fame of Commander Banks goes to his head, with the usual finale of all inflated egos. With a highly capable cast, a well-knit story and good stage settings, *Conflict* deserved a better fate than its few days of life on Broadway. There is some talk of reviving it, and this writer sincerely hopes this may be so."

On September 20, *Nigger Rich* (subtitled, *The Big Shot*) opened at the Royale Theater in New York City. Spencer Tracy played Eddie Perkins, the main supporting role. The play closed after eleven performances.

The Sam Harris production of a new play, *Dread*, by Owen Davis, opened in Washington, D.C., and then played on the subway circuit at the Majestic Theater in Brooklyn. In the cast with Mr. Tracy were Edwin Stanley, Miriam Boyle, Kathleen Comegys, Frank Shannon, George Meeker, Madge Evans, Marie Haynes, and Helen Mack. Tracy played a war hero who had distinguished himself on the battlefield by his courage and bravery, but who was a cad in private life. As he is about to marry a wealthy woman, an ex-wife turns up and warns the sister of the bride-to-be about Tracy's intentions. This younger sister, played by Madge Evans, threatens Tracy and says she will protect her sister.

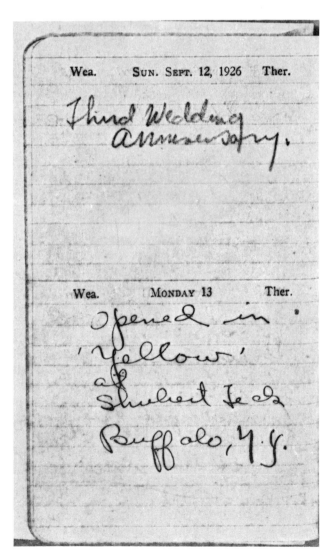

A page from Spencer Tracy's notebook

MISS Louise Treadwell, leading lady with the Wright Players, who open the stock season Sunday at the Faurot with "Laff That Off."

The Baby Cyclone, 1927

She dies, but returns to haunt Tracy, who goes insane. The play closed before it reached Broadway.

On November 12, a drama by Hugh Stange entitled *Veneer* opened at the Sam Harris Theater. Henry Hull, who played the leading character of Charlie Riggs, left the company and Tracy took over his role. After thirty-one performances the play closed.

Then, on January 15, 1930, a small news item appeared in *The New York Times* stating that Spencer Tracy was going to appear in a new play by John Wexley. The play about prison life was produced by Herman Shumlin, and opened in New Haven late in January under its original title, *All The World Wondered*. The name was changed to *The Last Mile* and the play opened on Broadway on February 13,, 1930.

Pat O'Brien later recalled the time of the opening in his autobiography:

> The big break seemed to have come for Spencer Tracy in *The Last Mile*. He was given the lead in the new play. It had an all-male cast, which to me seemed a little dangerous at the time. I recall Broadway had had few if any productions without the girls. Tracy returned glum and sagging from the break-in.
>
> "Boys, I'm in one helluva flop! I'd like to pull out, but I have a run-of-the-play contract."
>
> He pleaded with us. "Don't see the show—I've got no confidence in it." Spence had been honest when he told us he was in a flop. The tryout audience had been anything but responsive. "Their receptivity was as cold as the Yukon." Spence thought he was in a bomb.
>
> I bought a gallery ticket on opening night and witnessed a one-man performance of amazing power, of near-greatness—Spence as the condemned man. At the final curtain the audience stood and cheered. It was a spine-tingling production, the first of the powerful prison yarns. All the actors were fine, but Spence was an overnight sensation!

The Brooks Atkinson review of *The Last Mile* appeared in *The New York Times,* February 14, 1930. "By superimposing a desperate prison mutiny upon the normal ghastly routine of events in a death-house, the author of *The Last Mile* . . . has created a taut, searing drama with a motive. . . . It describes a roaring prison mutiny in which the condemned men visit upon their keepers the cold-blooded vengeance the State practices legally upon their kind. It is, in passing, a thesis play by the concrete method of comparisons. But first of all it is a drama of strength, resolution and horror. Mr. Wexley has let no thesis temper the forces of his dramatic writing. . . . Mears is a 'killer' acted with muscular determination by Spencer Tracy and acted well."

John Wexley, author of the play, later wrote:

> Tracy left the show temporarily during the summer months to do a film in Hollywood. Thomas Mitchell played the leading role during Tracy's absence and I believe gave a performance not as mannered and with more depth. I think Tracy was ex-

cellent in the role and, of course, he originated it—but, personally he never lived up to my conception of "Killer Mears." He was too much the "actor"—effective, but playing to the audience a good deal of the time and to that extent, self-conscious. He gave the character a sort of vanity or egotism, which should not have been present. I worked with him during the rehearsals on the reading or interpretation and he accepted direction gratefully from me which was very nice since I was considerably younger.

The play was a great success, and Spencer Tracy had reached the peak of theatrical honor.

In the late spring or early summer he made two short dramatic films for the Vitaphone Company at their studio in New York. Both films co-starred Katherine Alexander. The first, *Taxi Talks,* was released in June. The second, *The Hard Guy,* was released in September.

John Ford, while visiting New York, saw *The Last Mile.* He liked Tracy's performance and asked the Fox Film Corporation to hire Tracy for his film, *Up the River.* It was a one-picture contract; Tracy took a leave of absence from the play, and went to Hollywood alone to make the film, a comedy about prison life. It was the first feature-film appearance for both Spencer Tracy and Humphrey Bogart. When the studio executives saw the rushes they offered Tracy a long-term contract, to begin immediately. Tracy informed them he had agreed to complete the run of *The Last Mile.* They offered more money and said they could break his Broadway contract, but Tracy refused, and returned to New York City and his role in the play.

When the play closed, Tracy accepted a contract from Fox Films, and he, his wife, and son moved to Hollywood in November. They had their Thanksgiving Day dinner on the train going west. In the first three years in Hollywood (1931, 1932, and 1933) he made sixteen films. Years later he was to comment that any young actor seriously attempting to develop a career should do as much film work as possible, that limiting one's work to a single picture a year at an early stage in one's career was an unwise practice.

His second picture was *Quick Millions,* directed by a new and talented director, Rowland Brown, working with a fine script. It told the story of a man who used other people to gain power and money only to be destroyed by a member of his gang just as he reached the top. The other two pictures that year were *Six Cylinder Love,* the film version of a popular stage comedy; and *Goldie,* a romantic comedy based on an earlier film, and the first of three films that Tracy was to make with Jean Harlow.

In 1932 Spencer Tracy made eight films, co-starring with such stars as Joan Bennett, Sally Eilers, Doris Kenyon, Peggy Shannon, and Bette Davis. The films were *She Wanted A Millionaire, Sky Devils, Disorderly Conduct, Young America, Society Girl, Painted*

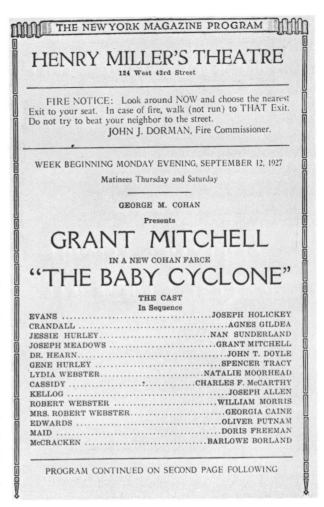

University of Texas

With his mother, Mrs. Carrie B. Tracy, his brother Carroll, his wife Louise, and his son John

The Tracys, John, Louise, Susie, and Spencer

Woman, Me and My Gal, and *Twenty Thousand Years In Sing Sing.*

On July 1, 1932, a daughter, Louise, was born to the Tracys. She was given the nickname of Susie and has been generally known by that name. The family now lived on a twelve-acre ranch that Tracy had purchased in the San Fernando Valley.

Spencer Tracy made five films in 1933. They were *Face in the Sky, Shanghai Madness, The Power and the Glory, The Mad Game,* and *A Man's Castle.*

The Power and the Glory was a strong film telling the life of a railroad magnate and his personal tragedy. The film begins with the main character's funeral and then flashes back to recount his life. The studio called this a new technique ("narratage"), and created a publicity campaign emphasizing the device, which, in fact, was not new. Preston Sturges made good use of the device in his original screenplay; however, the film succeeded not because of this device, but because of the good script, the outstanding direction by William K. Howard, and the fine performances by Colleen Moore and Spencer Tracy.

In the fall of 1933 Tracy made a film for Columbia Pictures called *A Man's Castle.* His co-star was the very young and lovely Loretta Young, already a veteran of many films. Frank Borzage directed this story of love in a shanty-town Depression camp.

The next film, *Looking for Trouble,* was the story of two telephone trouble-shooters who become involved with gangsters. Included in the dramatic climax of the film was the Long Beach earthquake. It was directed by William Wellman and co-starred Jack Oakie, Constance Cummings, and Arline Judge.

Tracy's second film in 1934 was *The Show-Off,* based on the George Kelly play. This was the third film version. Metro-Goldwyn-Mayer had planned to have Lee Tracy play the lead, but when he got into trouble with the Mexican government during the making of *Viva Villa,* L. B. Mayer fired him. Mayer tested several actors and then decided to borrow Spencer Tracy from Fox to play the part. Madge Evans co-starred, and the film was well directed by Charles F. Reisner. It gave Tracy an opportunity to play something different from his recent roles, and it was successful at the box office.

The other films that year were *Bottoms Up, Now I'll Tell,* and *Marie Galante.*

After making *It's A Small World* and *Dante's Inferno* in 1935, Tracy's contract with Fox Films was terminated. He then signed a contract with Metro-Goldwyn-Mayer. He made three suspense films for that studio: *Murder Man* and *Whipsaw* in 1935, and *Riffraff* in 1936. Then he made two films that changed his career and gave him the status of a major star.

44

Norman Krasna had written a story and Joseph Mankiewicz had worked on it. It told of an innocent man suspected of being a kidnapper who is nearly killed by a mob when they burn down the jail. The man escapes and hides, letting others think he is dead. His brothers and fiancée prosecute the members of the mob on the charge of murder. The embittered victim is willing to let the mob be sentenced to death for his supposed killing, but at the last minute he appears in court and they are freed. Sam Katz and Louis B. Mayer didn't like the story, thought it too harsh. But when Mankiewicz asked a second time, Mayer agreed to let him produce the film. Fritz Lang who had been in the United States several months waiting to do a film was asked to direct it. Spencer Tracy played Joe Wilson, the victim of the mob, and Sylvia Sidney played Katherine Grant, his fiancée. The film was made, with Mayer giving it his full backing as he usually did for any film that went into production so he would not be blamed for lack of support if a film failed at the box office. And *Fury* was not only successful at the box office, but was highly praised by many critics for its sociological commentary, with Lang receiving praise for the unremitting power of his direction.

Another film in production at the same time was the MGM spectacular *San Francisco,* starring Clark Gable, Jeanette MacDonald, Jack Holt, and Spencer Tracy. In this film Tracy had a supporting role, playing a priest. In an article in *The New York Times,* Frank Nugent said, "Mr. Tracy, late of *Fury,* is heading surely toward an award for the finest performance of the year." For his performance in *San Francisco* Tracy was nominated for an Academy Award, but Paul Muni won that year for his performance in *The Story of Louis Pasteur.*

His next film, *Libeled Lady,* gave Tracy a chance to do comedy again. His co-stars were Jean Harlow, Myrna Loy, and William Powell.

In 1937 he played the role of Manuel, a Portuguese fisherman in *Captains Courageous.* Victor Fleming directed the film, adapted from the Rudyard Kipling novel.

Spencer worked as hard as usual creating the character.

> I researched the accent for *Captains Courageous* and thought I'd worked up a beaut until they brought a *real* Portuguese-American fisherman to me. We sat down in the director's office and I tried out my exotic new accent on him. I said, "Now, would you say 'leetle feesh'?" and he said, "No, I'd say 'little fish.'" So in the film, I probably had the most un-Portuguese accent in history.

Spencer was hoping that the film would not be completed. "I was positive that I was doing the worst job of my life. I just felt sure I wouldn't surmount the singing, the dialect, and the curled hair."

The two other pictures he made in 1937 were *They Gave Him a Gun,* the story of a man who learned to kill in war and came home to kill in peacetime, in which Franchot Tone and Gladys George starred with him; and *The Big City,* in which he played a cab driver who marries an immigrant, played by Luise Rainer.

Joan Crawford recalls working with Spencer Tracy on his next film, the only film these two made together. In her autobiography, she said:

> *The Independent Film Journal* labeled me box-office poison. I was, at least, in excellent company. Also on the list were Marlene Dietrich, Fred Astaire, and Katharine Hepburn. MGM's answer was a new five-year contract, $1,500,000 a year, three pictures a year.
>
> My answer was *Mannequin,* with Spencer Tracy co-starring. Here was a down-to-earth story of a shopgirl who by intelligence and ambition rises from the slums to riches and happiness. Familiar? Yes, but this was a Mankiewicz production, and Joe has a genius for extracting the suds from soap opera. He brings to any production an honesty and power of approach. Our story was well told by Katherine Brush, the dialogue was direct, and conflict in the plot between capital and labor added dimension.
>
> I took one look at those poor Delancey Street sets and knew I was back home. I *was* Jessie—there was no trick in conveying her love, warmth, and ambition. And it was inspiring to play opposite Tracy. His is such simplicity of performance, such natural-

With Loretta Young on the set of A Man's Castle, *1933*

Spencer Tracy talking to young actors who were playing baseball between the shooting of scenes for A Man's Castle, *1933*

ness and humor. He walks through a scene just as he walks through life. He makes it seem so easy, and working with him I had to learn to underplay. We worked together as a unit, as if we'd worked together for years, yet there was also the extra little fillip of working with a new co-star, a powerful co-star. No matter how often you rehearse a scene, when the camera starts turning he surprises you with some intonation or timing so that your response is new and immediate.

When we got to the dancing scene the cameraman yelled, "Get closer. Get closer, Joan."

"I can't," I laughed. Spence was as solid as a rock and he wasn't thin. He promptly went on the black-coffee routine.

But most of the time the teasing was initiated by him. *Slug* I called him, from the day he was clowning around and took the stance of a boxer. In the most serious scene, Slug could break me up. As Jessie, I was supposed to be so serious about my life, my job; and as I spoke my lines, he'd watch me slyly, give that half grin of his, and rub his finger along his nose. I'd have to laugh. Take after take. But I learned. From Slug I learned to keep my own identity in a scene, not to be distracted by anything, including Tracy.

Columnists insisted we were feuding. We never had a moment's disharmony. He was considerate of me on the set.

On March 10, 1938, the tenth annual Academy Award dinner was held at the Ambassador Hotel. Spencer Tracy had received a nomination, but he was in the hospital. Mrs. Tracy attended the banquet. Louis B. Mayer stepped onto the stage and announced that Spencer Tracy had won the Academy Award for his

Madeleine Carroll visits Spencer Tracy and Helen Twelvetrees on the Fox set where Now I'll Tell *was being filmed, March 28, 1934*

46

Publicity picture with Sylvia Sidney for Fury, *1936*

the Glory, and down in the dumps when mediocre roles followed. Unfortunately, too many of his pictures belonged in the latter classification. He would disappear for days at a time on such occasions, and no one was able to locate him. Again and again he would be forgiven and start all over, only to become thoroughly discouraged. Finally he and the Fox company parted and many in Hollywood felt it was the end of what had been a promising career. But Spence was far from through. Metro signed him and started him in unpretentious pictures like *Murder Man* and *Whipsaw.* Instead of being a star himself, he was a leading man to all MGM's glamour girls. Spence never complained, but went to work with a will and finally, when *Fury* was released, it was apparent all he needed to return to stardom was the chance.

In April, *Test Pilot* was released. It was a popular film with Spencer Tracy, Clark Gable, and Myrna Loy working under the direction of Victor Fleming. Tracy was already at work on a film in which he would appear in one of the most remembered of his roles.

Some time before, a studio secretary had brought a magazine article to the attention of Eddie Mannix, who read it and sent it to John Considine, who read it and turned it over to Dore Schary to see if a film script could be written from the idea. The script, telling the struggles of Father Flanagan to found Boys Town, was written and Tracy was asked to play the part. He

role of Manuel in *Captains Courageous.* Mrs. Tracy went up onto the stage, accepted the Oscar and said: "I thank you for Spencer, Johnnie, Susie, and myself; and I want to tell all of you how much all of us appreciate it."

In a newspaper article of March 20, Louella Parsons discussed Spencer Tracy's career, his recent successes, and earlier difficulties.

A brief four years ago, Tracy was called the bad boy of Hollywood. The Fox executives were constantly at odds with him, because they considered him disobedient, lacking interest in his career, and unwilling to abide by the studio rules. I remember talking to him about that time, and I think I got an insight into his character. Spence wasn't really being a bad boy. He was only unhappy over the pictures that were being given him. Impulsive, and with all the human characteristics of the Irish, he was walking on air after a good picture like *The Power and*

With director Fritz Lang during the making of Fury, *1936*

During the filming of Captains Courageous

I Take This Woman had been in production for nearly three years. Josef von Sternberg had started the film, then it had been taken over by a second director, and finally W. S. Van Dyke reshot some portions and completed it. Spencer Tracy played opposite Hedy Lamarr in this picture, which was released early in 1940.

The first color film for both Spencer Tracy and director King Vidor was *Northwest Passage,* based on the first half of a novel by Kenneth Roberts. The studio writers were never able to complete the script for the second part. Difficult for all was the location shooting undertaken near McCall, Idaho. It was strenuous work, actors having to stand in the chilly water for hours of rehearsals and takes. Biting insects and tick fever made the work uncomfortable, especially for Tracy, who disliked all location work. The film was finished and released in February, 1940.

A year earlier MGM had made *Young Tom Edison* in which Mickey Rooney played the title role. It was decided to make a second film continuing the story of Edison from the age of twenty-five to the end of his career, with Spencer Tracy playing this difficult role. It had none of the color or excitement of roles such as Zola or Henry VIII (that actors Muni and Laughton played). But Howard Barnes in the New York *Herald Tribune* commented: "Edison is shown as an irascible, stubborn, insatiably curious man whose personal existence was exceedingly mundane, and whose profes-

Playing polo in the mid-1930's

wasn't sure he wanted to, since he had recently played a priest in *San Francisco.* But the studio convinced him and Tracy made the film. Tracy was also concerned about playing a living person. "I knew Father Flanagan personally, and felt nobody could put over his warmth, inspiration, and humaneness of feeling in a picture. But I became so absorbed in the characterization that by the end of the first week I had stopped worrying."

Early in 1939 Spencer Tracy accepted his second Academy Award for his performance as Father Flanagan in *Boys Town.* The same year Bette Davis also accepted her second Academy Award.

He made only one film in 1939, *Stanley and Livingstone.* Although Tyrone Power was originally slated to play the role of Stanley, for some reason Darryl Zanuck changed his mind and borrowed Tracy from MGM for the role. Kenneth Macgowen remembered in his book *Behind the Screen* that much location footage had to be rejected because a double for Power had been used and he was not a suitable double for Tracy. Director Henry King emphasized the historical authenticity of the period. Much location documentary footage was shot, for which Tracy read passages from Stanley's autobiography. Tracy had several long speeches; Stanley's final speech, in which he attempts to describe his adventures in Africa to the Royal Geographical Society, consisted of 442 words. Tracy's ability to make long speeches successful in a medium not suited to long speeches indicates the skill of his acting ability.

sional achievements defy dramatic projection. Nevertheless, by sheer persuasion of his acting Tracy makes the film definitely worth seeing. It is a relief to find an actor relying on his own artifice, not grease paint, to bring a great figure to life."

In June, 1940, Spencer Tracy returned to his alma mater, Ripon College, to receive an honorary degree. On that day Dean Graham said:

> Spencer Tracy, the world knows you as many people, for in your time you have played many parts. But Ripon College knows you in another role—that of the eager youth who spoke his lines impromptu to the cues of life. That youth we remember with affection, both for himself and for the great promise that he displayed, even then. That promise has been handsomely realized. Audiences all over the world have applauded your achievements, and that smaller—and more critical—audience of critics has twice granted you the distinction of the Academy Award. Such recognition bespeaks an acuteness of understanding, a breadth of sympathy, and a skill of artistry that belongs to the realm of creative culture. The task of the actor, as Shakespeare remarked, is, and ever has been, to hold the mirror up to nature to interpret the deepest passions of the human soul, and thereby to cleanse it through pity and terror in the classic Aristotelian sense. To that distinguished company you belong.

Boom Town was completed in 1940. It co-starred Clark Gable, Claudette Colbert, and Hedy Lamarr. Then, in 1941, Tracy made two more films: *Men of Boys Town;* and *Dr. Jekyll and Mr. Hyde,* in which Ingrid Bergman and Lana Turner also appeared.

Late in 1940 Spencer Tracy and Katharine Hepburn met for the first time to work in a film directed by George Stevens. The film was a delightful comedy called *Woman of the Year.* Little did the two stars realize at that time that they would become a popular screen couple and work together in eight more films.

The next year Tracy made *Tortilla Flat,* based on the Steinbeck novel, and *Keeper of the Flame,* with Hepburn. He also narrated *Ring of Steel,* a documentary that briefly presented the history of the United States Army from 1776 to 1942. The film, directed by Garson Kanin, was made by the Office of War Information.

In 1943, Tracy co-starred in *A Guy Named Joe,* along with Irene Dunne and Van Johnson. During the making of this film Van Johnson was in an auto accident. He has said that MGM would have replaced him (which would have seriously hurt his career) had not Tracy insisted that they shoot other scenes until Johnson was able to return to work.

The formal opening of the John Tracy Clinic was

With two polo-playing companions, Leslie Howard and Will Rogers

held in February of 1943. Founded in 1942, officially chartered in 1943, classes actually began in July of the later year. The clinic is the direct result of Mrs. Tracy's research into the subject of deafness in children and her hope of providing solutions to the problems encountered. The main purposes of the clinic are to (1) teach families of deaf children how to help them

Mrs. Tracy gives Spencer the Oscar she accepted on his behalf

Spencer Tracy with Father Flanagan, whom he portrayed in the film Boys Town

Spencer Tracy and Bette Davis accepting their Academy Awards in 1939 for the best performances by an actor and an actress in 1938

break the barrier of silence, (2) train teachers of the deaf, and (3) aid afflicted children themselves. Over the years this institution has developed into a world-renowned organization that has contributed much to a better understanding of deafness in children and has developed fine programs which can break down the silence that surrounds these children. The clinic's fall, 1962, bulletin said: "Mr. Spencer Tracy has backed his wife every step of the way in the development of the Clinic. Without his encouragement and support there could have been no John Tracy Clinic." Tracy made certain that his wife's concept became a practical reality. And this clinic, which has helped and will continue to help so many out of fear and silence, is Spencer Tracy's finest legacy.

Spencer Tracy inspects the Police Commissioners of Boys Town while on location filming Boys Town, 1938

In 1944, Spencer Tracy made two films: *The Seventh Cross,* and *Thirty Seconds Over Tokyo.* In 1945, he starred in *Without Love* with Katharine Hepburn.

Late in the summer of 1945, Tracy agreed to return to the Broadway stage in *The Rugged Path,* by Robert E. Sherwood.

The Burns Mantle theater annual, *The Best Plays of 1945,* noted the problems involved in the production. "The first months following the birth of *The Rugged Path* were rugged indeed. Spencer Tracy, one-time sturdy favorite of the Broadway drama, later on an even sturdier favorite of Hollywood drama, was announced for the leading role. Mr. Tracy, at first greatly enthused, later began to wonder if *The Rugged Path* was really the best drama he could find for a temporary return to the legitimate theatre. One day he was sure. The next day he wondered. The third day he consulted with friends. And finally he decided: he would take on the Sherwood drama for a sort of test flight, but with mental reservations. The tryouts in Providence, Washington and Boston brought mixed reviews. Tracy quit in Boston, walked out one night, but returned a few days later and went on with the play to New York City."

Staged by Garson Kanin, the play opened at the Plymouth Theater on November 10, 1945. In the cast were Martha Sleeper, Clinton Sundberg, Lawrence Fletcher, Henry Lascoe, Ralph Cullinan, Nick Dennis, Rex Williams, Jan Sterling, Theodore Leavitt, and Lynn Shubert. George Jean Nathan commented that Mr. Tracy "gave a performance that injected at least a superficial belief into the unbelievable materials provided him."

Revisions were made throughout the entire run. *The*

With director King Vidor during the making of Northwest Passage

Rugged Path closed after eighty-one performances.

The next year, 1946, was the first since he began making films that no film starring Spencer Tracy was released, although during much of that year he was working on *Sea of Grass* under Elia Kazan's direction. Katharine Hepburn, Melvyn Douglas, Phyllis

Spencer Tracy receives an honorary degree from Ripon College, June, 1940. Left to right: President S. Evans, Tracy, William Barber, J. Clark Graham, and H. P. Boody

51

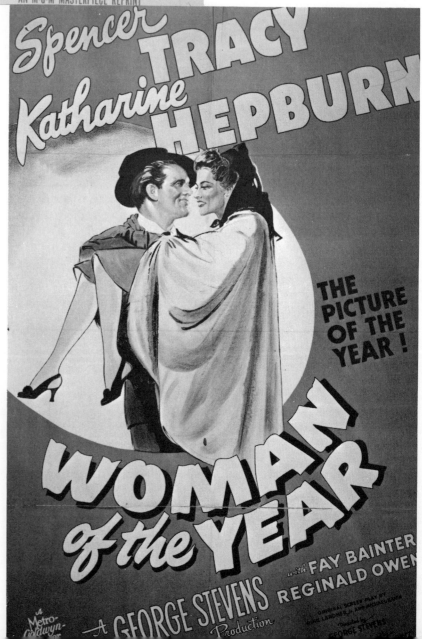

52

Thaxter, and Robert Walker appeared with him in this saga of the American West. The film was released in the spring of 1947. Later that year he made *Cass Timberlane* with Lana Turner.

The next year he again joined Katharine Hepburn in Frank Capra's production of *The State of the Union*, based on the Pulitzer-Prize-winning play by Howard Lindsay and Russell Crouse, which recounted the adventures of an honest politician involved with a corrupt political machine. Claudette Colbert was to have played the role of Mary Matthews, but she withdrew from the film, and Katharine Hepburn stepped in at the last minute to replace her.

In 1949 Tracy went to England to be directed by George Cukor and co-star with Deborah Kerr in the film version of actor Robert Morley's play, *Edward, My Son*. The film was not a success. George Cukor also directed Tracy's next film, but this time in Hollywood. Teamed with Katharine Hepburn for the sixth time, and co-starring Judy Holliday and Tom Ewell and David Wayne, with a script by Ruth Gordon and Garson Kanin, the film *Adam's Rib* proved most successful.

Early in 1950, *Malaya,* a melodrama set in southeast Asia, starring Spencer Tracy and James Stewart, was released. Later that year Tracy teamed up with Joan Bennett (she had worked with him in two Fox films in the early thirties) under the direction of Vin-

cente Minnelli to make *Father of the Bride*. Elizabeth Taylor played the daughter. The script, based on Edward Streeter's popular book, provided an entertaining picture.

The next year Metro-Goldwyn-Mayer followed this successful film with a sequel, *Father's Little Dividend,* again with Spencer Tracy, Joan Bennett, and Elizabeth Taylor playing the leading roles. That fall saw the release of Tracy's first film under the direction of John Sturges. It was a courtroom action film called *The People Against O'Hara*. Pat O'Brien, his old friend, had not worked for some time, and Tracy threatened to walk out unless the studio gave O'Brien a good part. The studio agreed, and the role did, in fact, reactivate O'Brien's career.

The Tracy family, Spencer, Susie, John, and Louise

53

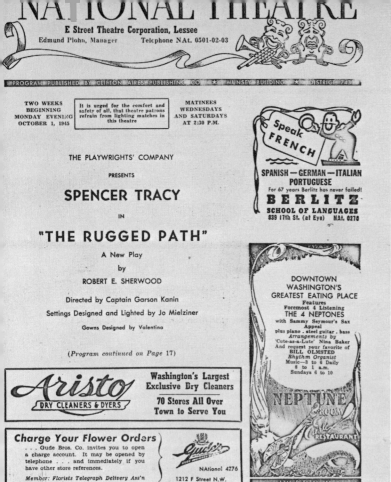

With Harry Rapf and Louis B. Mayer, MGM, 1940

Pat and Mike, another Tracy–Hepburn comedy, came out in 1952. Later that year Tracy played an unsympathetic character, the captain of the *Mayflower,* in Clarence Brown's spectacular production, *Plymouth Adventure.*

John, after graduating from college, and now working as an artist, was married in 1952. Louise and Spencer became proud grandparents when a son named Joseph Spencer Tracy was born to John and his wife in 1953.

The Actress opened on September 25, 1953. This film was based on a delightful book and play by Ruth Gordon drawn from her own life, which told of a girl's childhood in New England at the turn of the century, and her desire to become an actress. Tracy played the father, a former sailor now restricted to an unpleasant job, who watches his daughter mature and leave home.

Twentieth Century–Fox then asked Tracy to play the lead as Matt Devereaux in *Broken Lance.* It was an unusually well-written Western, beautifully photographed, and well directed by Edward Dmytryk. Also in the cast were Robert Wagner, Richard Widmark, Katy Jurado, Hugh O'Brian, Earl Holliman, and E. G. Marshall. The film was released in August, 1954.

Later that same year Tracy began work on *Bad Day at Black Rock,* in which he played a one-armed veteran who goes to a small desert community to give an honorary medal to a Japanese–American farmer, whose son had died in the war. The people of the town are antagonistic. Finally Tracy discovers that the *nisei* farmer was murdered by someone in the town. This tightly woven melodrama was based on an excellent script by Millard Kaufman, well directed by John Sturges, who made intelligent use of CinemaScope and offered Tracy in a role for which he was well suited, and for which he received an Academy nomination.

But it was the last film Tracy made for Metro-Goldwyn-Mayer. He was signed to appear in *Tribute to a Bad Man,* but arrived on location in the Colorado mountains after shooting had begun. There were arguments and conferences. Finally director Robert Wise asked that Tracy be replaced. The studio agreed. James Cagney took over the part, and production continued.

On location in France during filming of The Mountain

A photograph of three generations of the Tracy family. From left to right: John Tracy, Joseph S. Tracy, and Spencer Tracy

Tracy returned to Hollywood, and Metro-Goldwyn-Mayer released him from his contract and gave him a pension.

In 1956, Tracy made *The Mountain* under Edward Dmytryk's direction. Much of the film was shot on location in France near Chamonix. A comedy about office life followed in 1957. Co-starring Katharine Hepburn, Joan Blondell, and Gig Young, it was called *Desk Set*.

The next picture was *The Old Man and the Sea,* based on Hemingway's novel. The production had many problems. The filming ran over a year and the cost was forced up to a high of about $6,000,000. Director Fred Zinneman quit midway through production. John Sturges took over the work with its many headaches and completed it. Although Tracy was supposed to have one-third interest in the film, some said he was being difficult during the making, and yet disturbed that it was taking so long. "If I'd known what trouble it was going to be, I never would have agreed to do it," he said at the time.

It was an unusual film. Tracy was the only star in the film. He appears on the screen alone for about sixty out of the eight-six minutes running time, and he also speaks the off-screen narration. Unfortu-

Spencer Tracy and Ernest Hemingway visit during the filming of The Old Man and the Sea

nately, this film was not the work it might have been. The use of obvious studio tricks weakened its believability in spite of some very fine photography. The critics were not happy; but Tracy won another Academy nomination for his performance.

John Ford asked Tracy to play the political boss in his next film, *The Last Hurrah,* based on Edwin O'Connor's novel. The film captured a sense of Irish–American politics and provided heart-warming entertainment.

Spencer Tracy made no films in 1959.

In 1960, he began his association with director-producer Stanley Kramer, appearing in *Inherit the Wind.* The plot was based on a famous Tennessee trial. State law had forbidden the teaching of Darwinian evolution in the schools. When a teacher broke this law, some opponents with strong religious convictions took the case to court. Tracy played the defense attorney, based on the real-life attorney Clarence Darrow. Fredric March played the opposition leader, a character based on William Jennings Bryan. This film brought Tracy another Academy nomination.

In 1961 Tracy made two films. In Mervyn LeRoy's *The Devil at Four O'Clock,* he played an aging, alcoholic priest living on a small French island in the South Pacific, who has some convicts help him rescue the children and staff of a school on the island. Frank Sinatra was the co-star.

Judgment at Nuremberg was the second film under Stanley Kramer's direction. Tracy played a retired Maine judge who is asked to preside at the trial of four former Nazis. Others in the film were Burt Lancaster, Richard Widmark, Marlene Dietrich, Maximilian Schell, Judy Garland, and Montgomery Clift. Both Schell and Tracy were nominated by the Academy for best performance; and Maximilian Schell won the Oscar that year.

In 1963, Tracy narrated but did not appear in the MGM production of *How the West Was Won.* Then he appeared in the Stanley Kramer star-studded and rowdy spectacular, *It's A Mad, Mad, Mad, Mad World.* Because of illness, Tracy's contract limited his working day to six hours and specified no location work. On July 21, 1963, just as he was preparing to go on a picnic, he became ill with a congested lung condition. He was rushed to Saint Vincent's Hospital in Los Angeles, where he remained for several days. In December, John Ford offered Tracy a role in *Cheyenne Autumn.* Tracy wanted the role but was too sick to accept. The next year his health improved but he still didn't make any films, although he occasionally visited the studio sets.

Filming The Old Man and the Sea

He was to play a part in *The Cincinnati Kid,* but due to a relapse was unable to perform, so Edward G. Robinson took over the part.

In 1967 Spencer Tracy returned to work in his fourth film for Stanley Kramer. It was a delightful, topical comedy dealing with interracial marriage. Called *Guess Who's Coming to Dinner,* it also starred Katharine Hepburn, Sidney Portier, Katharine Houghton, Beah Richards, and Cecil Kellaway.

Just three weeks after completing the film, Spencer Tracy died of a heart ailment at his Hollywood Hills residence on June 11, 1967.

With Richard Widmark, Montgomery Clift, and Burt Lancaster during the filming of Judgment at Nuremberg, *1961*

A Captain Courageous

by BOSLEY CROWTHER

It is natural for a long-time moviegoer to wax senti-mental and sad over the death of a favorite actor whose intense and distinguished career has paralleled one's own growing older and provided many memorable joys. We all tend to weave into the fabric of our own experi-ences the self-identifications and emotional associations we have inevitably made with the actors and actresses whose characterizations we have especially enjoyed, so that their simulations of experience become, in a way, a part of ours.

This is a simple phenomenon that regularly occurs as a consequence of exposure to the devices of theater, and it needs no further exploration or extenuation here. We have our personal attachments to our favorite stars, and we feel a deep sense of general sadness and per-sonal loss when they die.

But the death of Spencer Tracy, whose passing a week ago came as no surprise to those aware of the pathetic erosion of his health, is sadly significant of something more than the departure of a personal favo-rite. It breaks one more strong and vibrant cable in the slowly crumbling bridge between motion pictures of this generation and the great ones of the past.

Mr. Tracy was of that order of robust and popular male stars brought into prominence and distinction in the first decade of talking films. They included Clark Gable, Gary Cooper, Humphrey Bogart, Wallace Beery, and Erroll Flynn, who have all been gathered to their maker, and James Cagney, Edward G. Robinson, and Fredric March, who are fortunately still with us, but not as active as they used to be. Mr. Tracy was one of those stalwart actors who were nurtured and spiraled to the top in the old star system the major studios promoted when they needed full ranks of contract players to per-form and adorn their many films.

Whatever the faults of that system—and there were many, including the fact that contract players were often forced to do pictures for which they had no quali-fications or taste—it did provide plenty of work for actors and give them plenty of chance to develop their skills and project the personalities they possessed.

How well we remember Mr. Tracy's surprising emer-gence in the role of the tough-quarter priest in *San Francisco* after a succession of unimpressive roles as gangsters and various other low-lifes, and his simulta-neous appearance as the innocent man who was ar-rested as a kidnapping suspect in *Fury* and was almost lynched by an agitated mob. He was forceful, honest, and impressive in these two dissimilar roles, and proved beyond any question that he was an actor to watch. But, of course, it was his brilliant performance as the Gloucester Portuguese fisherman in the film of Rud-yard Kipling's *Captains Courageous* that won for him the renown (and his first Oscar) that he so ably shoul-dered in a great variety of roles through thirty years.

With Freddie Bartholomew and John Carradine in Captains Courageous

With Mickey Rooney in Boys Town

The Motion Picture Academy of Arts and Sciences
Nominations and Awards

"Oscars don't mean a damn thing except as a gesture. That's what it has always meant, nothing more. It is given to you by friends. More than an award for ability, it is likely to be a sentimental award."

SPENCER TRACY

Spencer Tracy was nominated nine times for the best performance of the year by an actor. He won the Academy Award twice, first for his performance as Manuel in *Captains Courageous*, and second for his performance as Father Flanagan in *Boys Town*. He was the only actor to win Oscars in two consecutive years, for 1937 and 1938; just as Luise Rainer was the only actress to win twice in two consecutive years for her roles in *The Great Ziegfeld* (1936) and *The Good Earth* (1937). Spencer Tracy won more nominations than any other leading actor. Laurence Olivier won seven nominations and one Academy Award. Two actresses received more nominations: Bette Davis and Katharine Hepburn, each of whom won ten nominations. Both of these actresses won two Academy Awards. Nominated for the best picture of the year were the following five pictures in which Spencer Tracy starred: *Libeled Lady, Captains Courageous, Boys Town, Test Pilot,* and *Father of the Bride;* none of which won the year's award.

ACADEMY AWARD NOMINATIONS RECEIVED BY SPENCER TRACY

1. For the role of Father Mullin in *San Francisco*, MGM, 1936.
2. For the role of Manuel in *Captains Courageous*, MGM, 1937.
3. For the role of Father Flanagan in *Boys Town*, MGM, 1938.
4. For the role of Stanley Banks in *Father of the Bride*, MGM, 1950.
5. For the role of John J. MacCreedy in *Bad Day at Black Rock*, MGM, 1955.
6. For the role of the Old Man in *The Old Man and the Sea*, Warner Brothers, 1958.
7. For the role of Henry Drummond in *Inherit the Wind*, Stanley Kramer-United Artists, 1960.
8. For the role of Judge Dan Hayward in *Judgment at Nuremberg*, Stanley Kramer-United Artists, 1961.
9. For the role of Matt Drayton in *Guess Who's Coming to Dinner*, Columbia, 1967.

An Actor's Actor

by ED SULLIVAN

It was the annual Academy Award dinner, the banquet at which the Academy of Motion Picture Arts and Sciences announces to the world the selections of its members for the blue ribbons of the cinema industry. Glamour girls pecked glamorously at unglamorous squab chicken. Matinee idols regarded their wives sourly across the tables. Louis B. Mayer was called forward to acknowledge the Academy Award that had been voted to Spencer Tracy because of Spencer's performance in *Captains Courageous*.

You expected to hear the short studio executive exclaim about the genius that had won the prize for Tracy. You were apprehensive that the solemnity of the occasion might cause Mr. Mayer to hark back to Booth. "I'd like to praise first Spencer Tracy's sense of discipline," said Mr. Mayer. "Tracy is a fine actor, but he is most important to our studios because he understands why it is necessary to take orders from the front office, because he understands why it is wise to obey his directors, because he understands that when the publicity department asks him to cater to certain visitors it is necessary inconvenience."

The "historians" of the films, the columnists, have bruited it about that 38-year-old Spencer Tracy, bedded at the Good Samaritan Hospital in Hollywood on the epochal occasion, dissolved into tears when he learned that he had won the Academy Award. Far be it from this heckler to destroy the pathos of that scene, but I imagine that what they mistook for tears might have been gales of laughter. Tracy, if he thought back some years ago and remembered the caustic things said about him at that time, might well have chuckled at winning the Academy Award.

There was a time in Hollywood, when actors, envious of Tracy's capacity, both thespian and liquid, averred that he was headed for a no-good end. It was rumored that he was hard to handle, unreliable, given to baiting directors. Hollywood being a compound of envy and exaggeration, it is probable that much of this was overemphasized; but the fact remains that at one stage of his career Tracy would not have qualified for Mayer's "sense of discipline" acclaim. What makes the 1938 Academy Award winner worthy of panegyric is that, like Earl Sande's Stagehand, he got away to a slow start but overhauled his field and won out in a photographic finish.

There is another reason which leads me to believe that Tracy did not break down and cry in his hospital cot when late at night, as the story goes, they hammered at his door of pain and carried the news of victory. On the afternoon of the Academy banquet one of my "snoopers" phoned to report: "Mrs. Tracy is here at the hairdresser's, and she told the girl to do a particularly good job, because she will have to accept the Award by proxy tonight."

Mrs. Tracy scored a notable victory at the hair-

With Freddie Bartholomew in Captains Courageous

dresser's, because her coiffure was indeed elegant that night when she fulfilled her own prophecy by stepping out on the floor of the Biltmore Bowl and receiving the gold statuette. Luise Rainer had preceded her on the floor; and Luise, ever the emotional actress, accepted her award in a tremolo that was reminiscent of her telephone scene in *The Great Ziegfeld*. Actors and actresses at the banquet tables looked wryly at one another in wordless disapproval of Miss Rainer's opening of the emotional stops, but applauded politely. Into this breach stepped Mrs. Tracy. Charmingly and quite simply she said, "I accept this on behalf of Spencer, Susie, Johnny, and myself." She had not only "followed" Miss Rainer, but stopped the show. I've rarely heard such a thunder of applause as Mrs. Tracy won.

Commenting upon it in my column next day, I said that Mrs. Tracy had stolen the show and that she was "just the sort of person you expected Spencer Tracy's wife to be: simple and unaffected." Tracy immediately sent this wire:

"Dear Ed—Unable to express my appreciation for what you said about Louise. Just know it made me extremely happy. I shall always remember it. Best always, Spencer."

Tracy, sending that wire, must have been thinking back to Cincinnati, shortly after he first met Louise Treadwell. He proposed to her in a Cincinnati restaurant—and she said yes. You can doubt that these two, that gay night in Cincinnati, ever dreamed that some years later Louise would be accepting the greatest honor in filmdom for her husband and that his award and her speech would be telegraphed and wirelessed and cabled to every city desk of every newspaper in the world.

To render it more dramatic, just one week before the Academy Award dinner "someone" announced that Spencer Tracy and his wife were splitting up. So when, in accepting the gold statuette, she mentioned Susie and Johnny, everyone present got an immediate picture of

A scene from Boys Town

a family of four challenging the world to break it up. It was a very human moment in an affair that necessarily is cold and formal.

Not, mind you, that the glamour girls of Hollywood haven't tried to break up the Tracy alliance, just as they've tried to crack up every other marriage in which the husband or the wife offered an inviting target. More than one glamour girl has eyed Tracy with that come-hither look. The surprising part of it is that until the previous six months, Tracy's appeal had not registered on the screen. He was always rated a fine actor, but he was not a box-office draw. Theater managers, in explaining this, said that the girls from fourteen to twenty-one—the jury that makes a matinee idol—did not go for him in a big way. His fans were mostly men. But suddenly the girls of America started getting steamed up over Tracy, and with the feminine vote swinging on the ropes, Tracy scored with three great performances in *Fury, San Francisco,* and *Captains Courageous.*

Many reasons have been advanced for Tracy's sudden rise to the "box-office draw" classification. It is this observer's belief that world conditions had more than a little to do with it. In serious times the people want serious performers, and with the world in uproar Tracy was the one quiet, authoritative voice speaking from the screen. The girls turned to him as relief from the cocktail-shaking zanies who had been bouncing around the celluloid screen. That deduction is based on the mail that comes to a columnist's desk.

The turning point in Tracy's career arrived last November. That I sensed it first was not due to any psychic ability. I'd sold a news syndicate the idea of a national film plebiscite, to permit the fans to select their own favorite performers. Sixty-seven great newspapers all over the country conducted the balloting. To the amazement of Hollywood, Spencer Tracy finished fourth, not many votes behind Clark Gable, William Powell, and Robert Taylor.

I went out to the MGM studios, where Tracy was making *Mannequin* with Joan Crawford under Director Frank Borzage, and told him it looked certain that he'd finish up with the matinee idols. "Go on, you're kidding," Tracy retorted, wagging his pipe reprovingly. "Girls want those good-looking guys, but me—with this homely pan—" He shook his head eloquently. Right up to the day when the official results were printed, Tracy believed firmly that Clark Gable and I had concocted the whole thing as a "rib," which is stage slang for a hoax.

His suspicions of Gable were grounded in a guilty conscience, because no more facile "ribber" exists at MGM than Tracy. After the release of *Parnell,* in which Gable and Myrna Loy were panned unmercifully by the critics, Tracy had an instrument made to order. Working with Gable and Miss Loy in *Test Pilot,* Tracy made references to *Parnell* which were a source of constant hilarity. One afternoon Tracy was excused early and Gable called, "Good-by, you Milwaukee 'ham.' Forget to come back tomorrow too." Tracy was walking off the set, but he turned at the door and said, "Just remember, when I walk out of this door, all you have left is *Parnell.*" That he dodged the book Gable heaved at him was a tribute to Tracy's agility.

Just as Little Bill Johnson was a tennis player's idea of a tennis player, and just as Hornsby and Ty Cobb were "ballplayers' ballplayers," Tracy is an actor's actor. Gable, Miss Crawford, Myrna Loy, Jeanette MacDonald—all these have worked with him and they are unanimous in calling him the greatest trouper they've ever partnered. Directors tell you the same thing. He rarely blows up in his lines. He is what the profession calls "a quick study." He gets his lines quickly and reads them flawlessly.

You have undoubtedly noticed, in his performances, the ease with which Tracy acts. He underplays rather than overplays, is always in a minor key. In the middle of a dramatic line he'll scratch his nose or touch the lobe of his ear. These very natural gestures are part and parcel of his fine equipment of make-believe. His naturalness is his greatest asset. He carries it even to a refusal to use any makeup. "Whatever character I project is due to the lines in my forehead," he pointed out to an astonished director. "I'm homely, so there's no sense trying to make me a pretty-boy."

His delivery, low, effortless, and easy, makes him unique among Hollywood stars, for Tracy alone stands in no fear of "scene-stealers," those supporting players who bob up in a scene now and then and steal the picture from a star. Scene-stealers have no success with Tracy. Their tricks of gesture or voice are rendered harmless by his talent for underplaying a scene.

The FILMS

Up the River

1930

Produced and distributed by Fox. Director: John Ford. Production staged by William Collier, Sr. Original story and screenplay by Maurice Watkins. Photography: Joseph August. Editor: Frank Hull. Recording Engineer: W. W. Lindsay, Jr. Release date: October 12, 1930. Running time: 92 minutes.

The Cast

Saint Louis	Spencer Tracy
Judy	Claire Luce
Dannemora Dan	Warren Hymer
Steve	Humphrey Bogart
Jean	Joan Marie Lawes
Pop	William Collier, Sr.
Jessup	George MacFarlane
The Warden	Robert O'Connor

and Gaylord Pendelton, Goodee Montgomery, and Noel Francis

Synopsis

Saint Louis and Dannemora Dan, two hard-boiled criminals, are sent to prison. Also in prison is Steve and, in the woman's section, the girl he loves, Judy.

With Warren Hymer and Humphrey Bogart

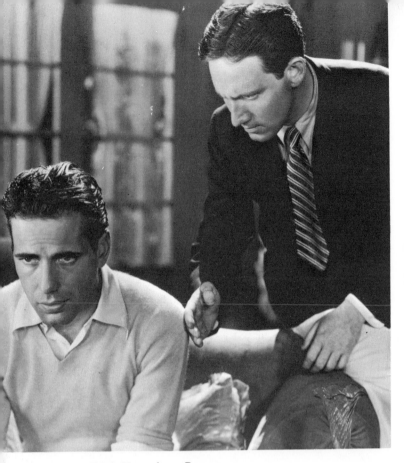

With Humphrey Bogart

*With Claire Luce and
Warren Hymer*

Steve is released and returns to his hometown where no one knows of his prison record. Frosby, a crooked salesman who framed Judy, follows Steve and threatens to expose his past unless Steve agrees to help him fleece the townspeople. Judy hears of Frosby's scheme and tells Saint Louis and Dan, who escape during a prison theatrical and go to Steve's rescue. By thwarting Frosby's plans, they save Steve's reputation, and then the two criminals return to prison.

*With Warren Hymer and
Humphrey Bogart*

70

With Marguerite Churchill

Quick Millions

1931

Produced and distributed by Fox. Director: Rowland Brown. Dialogue by C. Terrett, R. Brown, and John Wray. Scenario by Courtney Terrett and Rowland Brown, based on an original story by C. Terrett and R. Brown. Photography: Joseph August. Art Director: Duncan Cramer. Costumes: Sophie Wachner. Recording Engineer: W. W. Lindsay, Jr. Release date: May 3, 1931. Running time: 72 minutes.

The Cast

"Bugs" Raymond	Spencer Tracy
Dorothy Stone	Marguerite Churchill
Daisy de Lisle	Sally Eilers
"Arkansas" Smith	Robert Burns
Kenneth Stone	John Wray
"Nails" Markey	Warner Richmond
Jimmy Kirk	George Raft
Contractor	John Swor

Synopsis

Bugs Raymond, a truck driver, aspires to more wealth and turns to racketeering. He organizes the trucking associations and demands protection money. Through his activities he becomes a ruling force in the city. He decides to marry into society, choosing Dorothy Stone, who is in love with someone else. She rejects Raymond, and he plans to kidnap her on the wedding day with the help of his henchmen. But instead of helping him, his henchmen turn against him and take him "for a ride."

Article

"Some Gangster Films," by James Shelley Hamilton, *National Board of Review Magazine.*

Quick Millions is also the work of a newcomer, as promising a talent as has appeared in many a day. His name is Rowland Brown, and this is his first picture.

It would be a good picture made by anybody — it is exceptionally remarkable made by a young man before unheard of. It will probably not be a great box-office success: it is maybe too aloof and ironic and intellectual, without any of the quality known as "punch" to command mob attention. It demands an alert intelligence to follow its rapid movement and its unstressed implications, and a quick kind of sensitiveness that can respond more to deft and subtle suggestion than to emotional appeal. As a gangster picture it gets away from the liquor and gun-fighting that characterize most of such films, into the realm of racketeering that is deliberately big business, competing with legalized big business. The hero (played by Spencer Tracy) of it sets out quite definitely to be a big money power, not, as in *Little Caesar,* to gratify his ego by being king of the underworld, but through a purely intellectual concept of what power is, in modern society, and of how to obtain it. As he himself says, he is too nervous to steal and too lazy to work, but he has brains to think and plan with — so he builds up an organization that makes other people do the working and stealing that he can plan so capably, just as any money king builds up an organization.

Quick Millions also touches, as most gangster films make no pretense of doing, on what society might or ought to do about racketeering. *The Secret Six,* by its very title, pretended to discover a way of fighting gangsterdom, but it did it insincerely and wholly in the style of the old movie serials by using a version of the Hidden Hand as a *deus ex machina,* to step in and clean up the mess when the melodrama had run its allotted footage. *Quick Millions* at least suggests that businessmen and public opinion and district attorneys and judges have some responsibility in the matter, which is an extraordinary adult thing for a movie to do these days. But this film, aside from being the most intelligent of the gangster films, is probably most important for being the debut of a director who has a fresh and individual cinematic talent which will be exciting to watch.

. . . One final word about gangster pictures: none of them solves any problems. They are merely entertainment, of a particularly up-to-the-minute and exciting kind. They provide nothing but thrills and horrors, and some amusement, beyond what other movies provide. Until they admit, for instance, that some of our largest and most respectable fortunes are founded on racketeering as essentially anti-social and iniquitous as Al Capone's, they will get nowhere near a diagnosis of what this hugely headlined evil really is. And until they understand the evil they cannot find a cure for it — they will be merely what they now are, a sensational pastime.

With Sally Eilers

With Lorin Raker and Sidney Fox

Six Cylinder Love

1931

Produced and distributed by Fox. Director: Thornton Freeland. Screenplay by William Conselman and Norman Houston, based on a play by William Anthony McGuire. Photography: Ernest Palmer. Editor: J. Edwin Robbins. Sound Engineer: Albert Pratzman. Release date: May 10, 1931. Running time: 79 minutes.

The Cast

William Donroy	Spencer Tracy
Monty Winston	Edward Everett Horton
Marilyn Sterling	Sidney Fox
Richard Burton	William Collier, Sr.
Margaret Rogers	Una Merkel
Gilbert Sterling	Lorin Raker
Stapleton	Willian Holden
Mrs. Burton	Ruth Warren
Harold Rogers	Bert Roach
Janitor	El Brendel

Synopsis

A young couple, Marilyn and Gilbert Sterling, acquire an expensive car and then trouble begins: Several sponging friends hang around just for the rides and the parties; the wife has a smash-up and damage claims follow; the husband appropriates $5,000 from his employer to pay the damages. A solution to their mounting problems is found when the goofy janitor buys their car. The debt can be repaid and the car, the source of all the problems, is gone.

Review

Mordaunt Hall, *The New York Times*

. . . Mr. Tracy's impersonation is so satisfactory that the only complaint that can be offered is that one does not see enough of him.

With El Brendel

Goldie

1931

Produced and distributed by Fox. Director: Benjamin Stoloff. Scenario and dialogue by Gene Towne and Paul Perez. Photography: Ernest Palmer. Editor: Alex Troffey. Release date: June 28, 1931. Running time: 68 minutes.

With Jean Harlow and Warren Hymer

With Jean Harlow

With Warren Hymer

The Cast

Bill	Spencer Tracy
Spike	Warren Hymer
Goldie	Jean Harlow
Gonzales	J. DeVorska
Wife	Leila Karnelly
Husband	Ivan Linow
Constantina	Lina Basquette
Russian Girl	Eleanor Hunt
Dolores	Maria Alba
Barker	Eddie Kane

Synopsis

Spike, a sailor, finds a book of girls' addresses. When he dates these girls, he finds that each is tattooed. Spike hopes to find the man who left these marks of his conquest and give him a beating. But when he meets his adversary, Bill, also a sailor, Spike becomes a friend of his instead.

In Calais, Spike falls in love with Goldie, a high-diver at a carnival. Bill warns Spike that Goldie just wants his money. Spike doesn't believe him. Goldie tries to win Bill over, but he is not taken in. Later when Spike discovers Bill's tattoo mark on Goldie, his eyes are opened and he walks out on her.

75

She Wanted a Millionaire

1932

Produced and distributed by Fox. Director: John Bly-stone. Dialogue Director: William Collier. Scenario by William A. McGuire, based on a story by Sonya Levien. Photography: John Seitz. Editor: Ralph Dixon. Musical Director: George Lipschultz. Sound Recording: C. Clayton Ward. Release date: February 21, 1932. Running time: 80 minutes.

The Cast

Jane Miller	Joan Bennett
William Kelley	Spencer Tracy
Mary Taylor	Una Merkel
Roger Norton	James Kirkwood
Mrs. Miller	Dorothy Peterson
Mr. Miller	Douglas Cosgrove
Humphrey	Donald Dillaway

and Lucille LaVerne and Tetsu Komai

Synopsis

Jane Miller, a poor girl, sets out to marry a millionaire. A vicious millionaire, Roger Norton, finds her winning a beauty contest in Atlantic City. But William Kelley, a breezy newspaperman, also loves her and warns her not to go away with Norton. Nevertheless, Jane goes with Norton to his château in France. He persecutes her, making sinister advances. He is finally prevented from killing her when one of his own servants kills him. Jane returns to Kelley.

With Joan Bennett and James Kirkwood

*With William Boyd and
Ann Dvorak*

Sky Devils

1932

*Distributed by Caddo–United Artists. Producer: How-
ard Hughes. Director: Edward Sutherland. Scenario by
Joseph March and Edward Sutherland. Dialogue by
Robert Benchley, Joseph March, James Starr, Carroll
Graham, and Garrett Graham. Original story by Joseph*
*Moncure March and Edward Sutherland. Photography:
Gaetano Gaudio. Music by Alfred Newman. Record-
ing Engineer: William Fox. Release date: March 12,
1932. Running time: 90 minutes.*

*With William Boyd and
Ann Dvorak*

The Cast

Wilkie	Spencer Tracy
Sergeant Hogan	William Boyd
Mitchell	George Cooper
Mary	Ann Dvorak
The Colonel	Billy Bevan
Fifi	Yola D'Avril
The Innkeeper	Forrester Harvey
The Captain	William B. Davidson
The Lieutenant	Jerry Miley

Synopsis

Wilkie and Mitchell, a pair of buddies, formerly lifeguards who couldn't swim, are drafted into the army, and in trying to desert, stow away on a transport that brings them into the war zone. There they meet the familiar, hardboiled sergeant, Sergeant Hogan, who makes their life miserable. Battling over a girl while A.W.O.L., they accidently destroy an enemy ammunition dump. They return to their own lines as heroes. But when Wilkie and Mitchell demonstrate how they wrecked the German outfit, they cause havoc in their own lines.

With William Boyd and Ann Dvorak

With George Cooper

78

Disorderly Conduct

1932

Produced and distributed by Fox. Director: John W. Considine, Jr. Original story and screenplay by William Anthony McGuire. Photography: Ray June. Musical Director: George Lipschultz. Art Director: Duncan Cramer. Costumes: Guy S. Duty. Release date: March 20, 1932. Running time: 82 minutes.

The Cast

Phyllis Crawford	Sally Eilers
Dick Fay	Spencer Tracy
Olsen	El Brendel
Tom Manning	Ralph Bellamy
James Crawford	Ralph Morgan
Tony Alsotto	Frank Conroy

and Dickie Moore, Alan Dinehart, Claire Maynard, C. Keefe, Nora Lane, Geneva Mitchell, Charles Grapewin, James Todd, and Sally Blane

With Ralph Morgan

With El Brendel

Synopsis

Motorcycle officer Dick Fay gives Phyllis Crawford a ticket for speeding, but she only laughs at him, for her father is influential, much of his revenue coming from graft. Because of the arrest Fay is demoted to a walking patrolman under Tom Manning, the captain. Soured by his experience, Fay makes a fool of his captain, who is in love with Miss Crawford. Fay then tips off gangster Alsotto that Manning plans a raid. However, Manning discovers what Fay has done, and forces him to lead the raid on Alsotto's place. During the raid Fay discovers Miss Crawford, helps her escape, and then uses this knowledge to blackmail her father. Alsotto is released from jail and hunts Fay to kill him. Fay's nephew is killed instead, but Fay kills Alsotto. The boy's death deeply affects Fay, who confesses to Captain Manning, and returns the blackmail money. Dick Fay is returned to his motorcycle post.

With Doris Kenyon

Young America

1932

Produced and distributed by Fox. Director: Frank Borzage. Assistant Director: Lew Borzage. Screenplay by William Conselman, based on a play by John Frederick Ballard. Photography: George Schneiderman. Musical Director: George Lipschultz. Recording Engineer: Eugene Grossman. Release date: April 17, 1932. Running time: 70 minutes.

The Cast

Jack Doray	Spencer Tracy
Edith Doray	Doris Kenyon
Arthur Simpson	Tommy Conlon
Judge Blake	Ralph Bellamy
Grandma Beamish	Beryl Mercer
Mrs. Taylor	Sarah Padden
Patrolman Weems	Robert Homans
Nutty	Raymond Borzage

and Dawn O'Day, Betty Jane Graham, Louise Beavers, Spec O'Donnell, William Pawley, and Eddie Sturgis

With Doris Kenyon

Synopsis

Arthur and Nutty, two young boys who have gotten into trouble with the law, are paroled by the judge to Mrs. Taylor, Arthur's dour and bitter aunt. The boys spend one night with Nutty's grandmother, who is stricken with an illness. The boys make a futile attempt to awaken the druggist for the needed medicine, but when their attempt fails, they break into the drugstore and steal the medicine. Arthur is caught by the police. Both boys lie to save each other, but when the police talk to the grandmother, they tell the truth. Mrs. Taylor, angered, refuses to take them back. Mrs. Doray, the druggist's wife, asks for custody of Arthur over her husband's objections. Left alone one night, Arthur takes some money to help save Nutty's life, but Nutty dies anyway. When Arthur returns home he finds the Dorays fighting about him and he runs away. When he finally returns, he finds Mr. Doray being held up in the drugstore, and in attempting to help is taken by the bandits as a hostage. However, Arthur wrecks the getaway car and the bandits are captured. Finally, Mr. Doray agrees to keep the boy and decides to adopt him.

With Doris Kenyon

With James Dunn

Society Girl

*With Peggy Shannon and
James Dunn*

1932

*Produced and distributed by Fox. Director: Sidney
Lanfield. Scenario by Elmer Harris, based on a play by
John Larkin, Jr. Photography: George Barnes. Editor:
Margaret Clancy. Musical Director: George Lipschultz.
Art Director: Gordon Wiles. Sound Recording: W. W.
Lindsay, Jr. Release date: May 29, 1932. Running
time: 67 minutes.*

The Cast

Johnny Malone	James Dunn
Judy Gelett	Peggy Shannon
Briscoe	Spencer Tracy
Warburton	Walter Byron
Curly	Bert Hanlon
Alice Converse	Marjorie Gateson
Miss Halloway	Eula Guy Todd

With Peggy Shannon

84

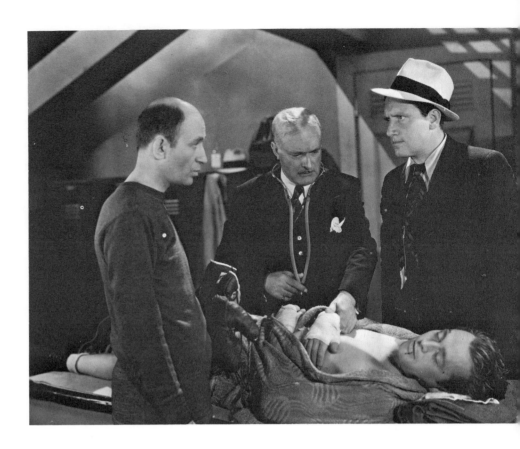

Synopsis

Johnny Malone, prizefighter, is training for a championship fight when Judy Gelett arrives and takes his mind entirely off his work. Briscoe, Johnny's manager, tries to warn him, finally becomes annoyed, and walks out on Johnny just before the big fight. Then Judy walks out on Johnny, and he loses the fight.

With Peggy Shannon

*With Peggy Shannon and
William Boyd*

Painted Woman

1932

Produced and distributed by Fox. Director: John Blystone. Screenplay by Guy Bolton and Leon Gordon, based on a play by Alfred C. Kennedy. Photography: Ernest Palmer. Editor: Alex Troffey. Musical Director: George Lipschultz. Musical Score: Arthur Lange and Hugo Friedhofer. Recording Engineer: Eugene Grossman. Release date: August 21, 1932. Running time: 73 minutes.

The Cast

Tom Brian	Spencer Tracy
Kiddo	Peggy Shannon
Captain Boynton	William Boyd
Robert Dunn	Irving Pichel

and Paul Roulien, Murray Kinnell, Laska Winter, C. Martin, Paul Porcasi, Stanley Fields, Wade Boteler, Jack Kennedy, and Dewey Robinson

Synopsis

Kiddo is an entertainer in a Singapore nightclub. Captain Boynton plans to marry her. Kiddo becomes involved in a killing. In order to escape she lies to Boynton, who takes her on his ship. When he discovers the truth he leaves her on a South Sea island. There Kiddo meets Tom Brian, falls in love with him, tells him the truth about her past, and they marry. During another voyage, Boynton returns, is furious that Kiddo has married, and is killed by Tom's native servant. Kiddo is accused of the crime and goes on trial. Tom also thinks her guilty and walks out on her, but when the native boy confesses the crime all is set right.

Peggy Shannon

86

With Joan Bennett

With Joan Bennett

Me and My Gal

1932

Produced and distributed by Fox. Director: Raoul Walsh. Assistant Director: Horace Hough. Screenplay by Arthur Kober, based on a story by Barry Connors and Philip Klein. Photography: Arthur Miller. Art Director: Gordon Wiles. Recording Engineer: George Leverett. Release date: December 4, 1932. Running time: 79 minutes.

The Cast

Dan	Spencer Tracy
Helen	Joan Bennett
Kate	Marion Burns
Duke	George Walsh
Pop	J. Farrell MacDonald
Baby Face	Noel Madison
Sarge	Henry B. Walthall
Jake	Bert Hanlon
Allen	Adrian Morris
Eddie	George Chandler

Synopsis

Dan, a young cop, has a beat on the New York waterfront. There he meets Helen, a waitress, and a romance develops. Kate, Helen's sister, gets involved

With Joan Bennett

with Duke, a gangster. Just in time, Dan captures Duke, saving Kate, Then Helen and Dan decide to marry.

Review

Aaronson, *Motion Picture Herald*

Contributing immeasurably to the ultimate result in the film are the performances of Spencer Tracy and Joan Bennett as the cop and his girl. As a matter of fact, the two "make" the picture. Tracy with his slangy, "wisecracking" vocabulary and his easy, happy-go-lucky role does a splendid job; which is matched, letter for letter, by that of Miss Bennett, who is a sheer delight.

With Joan Bennett

With Lyle Talbot

20,000 Years In Sing Sing

1932

Produced and distributed by Warner–First National. Director: Michael Curtiz. Associate Director: Stanley Logan. Screenplay by Courtney Territt, Robert Lord, Wilson Mizner, and Brown Holmes, based on the book by Lewis E. Lawes. Photography: Barney McGill. Editor: George Amy. Musical Director: Leo F. Forbstein. Musical Score: Bernhard Kaun. Art Director: Anton Grot. Costumes: Orry-Kelly. Release date: December 24, 1932. Running time: 81 minutes.

The Cast

Tom Connors	Spencer Tracy
Fay	Bette Davis
Bud	Lyle Talbot
Mr. Long (Warden)	Arthur Byron
Dr. Ames	Grant Mitchell
Hype	Warren Hymer
Finn	Louis Calhern

and Sheila Terry, Edward J. McNamara, Spencer Charters, Sam Godfrey, Nella Walker, Harold Huber, William LeMaire, Arthur Hoyt, George P. Collins, Rockliffe Fellows, Lucille Collins, Clarence Wilson, and Jimmie Donlon

Synopsis

Tom Connors is sent to prison. But he refuses to conform to the rules and is put in solitary confinement. He changes, passes up an opportunity to escape, and is given more consideration. When his girl is seriously hurt in an auto accident, he is given a 24-hour leave to see her. While on leave, he kills Finn, who is responsible for his being in prison and now for the death of Fay. Keeping his promise, he returns to prison to die for his crime.

Review

McCarthy, *Motion Picture Herald*

. . . If you have seen *I Am a Fugitive from a Chain Gang,* you can appreciate the quality of Spencer Tracy's acting, inasmuch as it is fully on a par with Paul Muni's for effectiveness and pulling his auditors along with him.

With Arthur Byron and Bette Davis

With Marian Nixon

Face in the Sky

1933

Produced and distributed by Fox. Director: Harry Lachman. Screenplay by Hymphrey Pearson, based on a story by Myles Connolly. Photography: Lee Garmes. Dialogue Director: William Collier, Jr. Musical Director: Louis De Francesco. Musical score by Peter Brunelli, R. H. Bassett, Hugo Friedhofer, and J. S. Zamecnik. Songs by Val Burton and William Jason. Settings: William Darling. Wardrobe: David Cox. Recording Engineer: E. Clayton Ward. Release date: January 15, 1933. Running time: 77 minutes.

The Cast

Joe Buck	Spencer Tracy
Madge	Marian Nixon
Lucky	Stuart Erwin
Triplet the Great	Sam Hardy
Ma Brown	Sarah Padden
Jim Brown	Frank McGlynn, Jr.
Pa Brown	Russell Simpson

and Billy Platt, Lila Lee, and Guy Usher

Synopsis

Joe Buck, a wandering sign painter and the best in his line, travels about New England with his partner, Lucky, finding jobs where they can. Painting a large sign on the side of a barn, Joe can't find the right expression for a face. Madge appears and Joe copies her smile. Later, Madge hides in their wagon, and when the painters finish the sign they depart. Joe and Lucky are arrested for kidnapping, but when Madge promises to marry Joe, the charges are dropped. Then Joe meets the challenge of his life, when he goes to New York City to paint a mammoth sign that has been a stumbling block to many other painters. After difficulties, he finally succeeds.

90

*With Marian Nixon and
Stuart Erwin*

With Marian Nixon

With Fay Wray

Shanghai Madness

1933

Produced and distributed by Fox. Director: John Blystone. Screenplay: Austin Parker. Adaptation: Gordon Wellesley. Original story: Frederick Hazlitt Bren- *nan. Photography: Lee Garmes. Musical Director: Samuel Kaylin. Recording Engineer: W. W. Lindsay, Jr. Release date: Aug. 4, 1933. Running time: 68 minutes*

With Fay Wray and Eugene Pallette

With Fay Wray

The Cast

Pat Jackson	Spencer Tracy
Wildeth Christie	Fay Wray
Li Po Chang	Ralph Morgan
Lobo Lonergan	Eugene Pallette
First Officer Larsen	Herbert Mundin
William Christie	Reginald Mason
Van Emery	Arthur Hoyt
Rigaud	Albert Conti
Mrs. Glissen	Maude Eburne
Von Uhlenberg	William von Brincken

Synopsis

During the 1920s in China, Lieutenant Pat Jackson attacks and destroys a Chinese post. For violating neutrality, he is court-martialed and discharged from the Navy. No one will give him a job. Then he saves the life of Wildeth. The Mandarin hires him to run a riverboat carrying guns and supplies. Wildeth, contrary to her father's wishes, follows Pat, hiding on the boat to be with him. Stopping at a mission, Wildeth is left in Mrs. Glissen's care. Later, when the boat returns, the mission is under siege from a Communist band. Pat drives the attacking band away, and saves the mission. Because of his heroism, he is restored to the Navy, and Wildeth's father now agrees to a wedding for his daughter and Pat.

The Power and the Glory

1933

Distributed by Fox. Produced by Jesse L. Lasky. Director: William K. Howard. Original screenplay by Preston Sturges. Photography: James W. Howe. Musical Director: Louis De Francesco. Musical score by J. S. Zamecnik, Peter Brunelli, and Louis De Francesco. Art Director: Max Parker. Costumes: Rita Kaufman. Recording Engineer: A. W. Protzman. Release date: October 6, 1933. Running time: 76 minutes.

The Cast

Tom Garner	Spencer Tracy
Sally	Colleen Moore
Henry	Ralph Morgan
Eve	Helen Vinson

and Clifford Jones, Henry Kolker, Sarah Padden, Billy O'Brien, Cullen Johnston, and J. Farrell MacDonald

Synopsis

After the funeral of Tom Garner, railway president, his private secretary describes the man's life. It is a story of the disaster and failure that may come as the aftermath of an overpowering struggle for success. Starting as a track walker, Garner moves through the various jobs in the railway company until he becomes president. Too busy at work, Garner doesn't notice that his own son has fallen in love with his second wife. When he discovers what has happened, his private life is destroyed.

Comment

"A Remembrance" by Jesse Lasky, from his autobiography *I Blow My Own Horn,* written with Don Weldon (Doubleday & Co., Garden City, N. Y., 1957).

At Fox I also made the *Warrior's Husband, I Am Suzanne, The Power and the Glory,* in which a comparatively unknown actor, Spencer Tracy, made a smash hit.

I brought Hector Turnbull to Fox as my story editor and associate producer. While in Europe scouting for material Hector found an American writer he thought had possibilities, Preston Sturges, who had

With Colleen Moore

authored the play *Strictly Dishonorable* and had an idea for a picture, though, to my knowledge, he had never written for pictures.

I sent for Sturges when he returned from abroad and asked him to tell me the story that had intrigued Hector.

"It isn't a story I can tell very well. It's too episodic," he said, "but I'll write it."

I raised my eyebrows at that. He obviously wasn't wise to the ways of Hollywood in a day when so many original stories were sold in ad-lib form over a luncheon or in a conference before being committed to paper. But I had no objection to reading the idea instead of listening to it. I knew that if it had any merit I could put a team of two or four or a half-dozen skilled film writers on it to develop the basic idea in a manner suitable to the film medium.

Preston Sturges went away and wrote his story. And he didn't even know enough about screen-writing to know that the first step is to do a *treatment,* or narrative story line. That's what I expected him to bring back, a few pages synopsizing the plot. Instead, he brought a screen play of proper length, complete to every word of dialogue, the action of every scene blueprinted for the director, and including specific technical instructions for the cameraman and all departments.

He told the story in flashback, starting with the death of his subject, an unprecedented screen technique then but later used with powerful effect by Orson Welles and others. The manuscript crackled with its originality of conception and craftsmanship.

I was astounded. It was the most perfect script I'd ever seen. I dispensed with the usual practice of having other writers go over a finished script "with a fresh mind" to make improvements. I wouldn't let anyone touch a word of it. The director, William K. Howard, shot *The Power and the Glory* just as Preston Sturges wrote it.

I've heard Spencer Tracy tell people he wouldn't be a film star today if it hadn't been for me. He might not have become a star so quickly if I hadn't given him one of the year's choicest roles in *The Power and the Glory,* but with a talent like his I'm sure he would have reached the heights just the same. I make no claim to discovering him. He had given a notable performance in *The Last Mile* on the stage and impressed the Fox people enough that they put him under contract. I did, however, help him get his career started off on the right foot by being a little tolerant and giving him a second chance after he muffed his first one.

I had slated him for the starring role in *Helldorado.* Just as the picture was ready to roll, Spence disappeared. The studio gumshoed all the bars but couldn't find him.

With Colleen Moore

Postponing the scheduled starting date of a picture is sometimes prohibitively costly if not downright impossible because of interlocked commitments geared to a timetable. In this case we couldn't even shoot around our star until he showed up because he had to be in almost all the scenes. We slapped Richard Arlen into the part, which didn't fit him at all, but there was no time to tailor it to his personality.

The studio rounded up Tracy a few days later and I sent word to him that I would never ask him what happened but that it might have happened to me instead of him and I was glad it didn't so I was willing to forget it. I added that there were plenty more good parts and I wanted to see him, but not till he had taken a little vacation and pulled himself together. He went to Honolulu and then reported back to the studio scared stiff, but not stiff.

"Spence, you look great!" I greeted him. "I've got

a hell of a part for you!" and we put him in *The Power and the Glory*.

I'm not suggesting that the best way to become a movie star overnight is to forget to report for work on your first assignment. There are clauses in contracts by which the studio can drop a player like a hot potato over such an incident. Holding up production is the unforgivable sin in Hollywood. Players have been suspended, well-launched careers have been cut short by undependability and indiscretions. And Tracy's career was just beginning. The studio could even have sued him for damages.

I don't know to this day whether it was exuberance, lack of confidence, or personal problems that caused his lapse, because I never asked him. But I knew somehow in a way I can't explain that if I overlooked it, it wouldn't happen again. He's one of those who would go out of his way for me.

Review

William Troy, *The Nation*

Interesting for a number of different reasons, *The Power and the Glory* will be found chiefly interesting for its attempt to introduce a new narrative technique to the screen. The story opens with what is really its conclusion—the funeral services of the hero, a great railroad executive, who has killed himself and whose memory is reviled by all but one of the people who have known him. This one is his former secretary, a boyhood friend to whom he has always been kind, and who as a result defends his reputation. By relating to his wife all the steps in the dead man's career, from the time he was a rail walker in the West to his days of "power and glory," he [the secretary] tries to show her that the opinion the world had of him was false and uncomprehending. The method used to retrace the past is not the old-fashioned flashback, which once established always continued for a time without shifting back to the present, but rather a rapid and skillful juxtaposition of recent events in the hero's life with the remoter events that explain them. Most of the scenes, of course, are projected directly with dialogue and action, but certain of them, distinguished by a semi-fade-out in the lighting, represent what are supposed to be re-creations of the narrator's own memory or

imagination. The narrator supplies the transitions, marks the contrasts, and interprets what is happening. A mixture of dramatic action and recited narrative, the result has much in common with the earliest Greek plays, in which the leader of the chorus had much the same function as the narrator in the film. But "narratage," as the Fox Company has dubbed the method, has a closer parallel in a variety of novel technique perfected long ago by Henry James and illustrated in its more popular mutations in the fiction of Joseph Conrad. It is not possible to review all the advantages that the so-called "oblique point of view" had for these novelists—that of supplying an interpretation of events not by the author was only one of them; but the purpose behind it was clearly to show that reality is a much more complex thing than novels and plays usually make it out to be. What made Conrad have his Marlow tell Lord Jim's story in such a tortuous and apparently capricious manner was the desire to communicate Jim's "inscrutable" mystery to us exactly in the order in which it was revealed to one man—therefore, not in any systematic order, but in unexpected flashes that were like "rifts in a fog." The same impulse is behind the technique of *The Power and the Glory,* and the result is that Spencer Tracy's railroad president is one of the fullest characterizations ever achieved on the screen. At the same time, few pictures have offered so

much interest in their sheer construction, which is another and different result of the method. "Narratage," therefore, opens possibilities to the screen of combining the methods of both the drama and prose fiction. Its only danger is the danger of any method—that of being misused; and it must be recalled that as used in fiction it seemed to lead to a certain indifference toward subject matter—in James to an increasing tenuity of substance, in Conrad to an ever cruder romanticism. Neither of these charges, however, can be made against the picture which introduces it to the screen: its subject is the great American Myth, and its theme is futility. Even five years ago such a parable of the self-made American businessman being pressed on by a hard-driving, power-mad American female to misery and self-destruction would have been too much for the movie public to stomach. Now its elements have been so well absorbed that interest can be directed to what is made of them. In other words, *The Power and the Glory,* if it is not satisfactory in all its details, answers to most of what we expect of a work of art.

Newsweek

"Narratage," what is it? Whatever it is, Fox Film Company announces that it has been employed in *The Power and the Glory.*

"Once in a very long while something new appears," says Jesse Lasky in the program. *"The Power and the Glory* is the first 'narratage' screenplay ever made. It embodies the action of the silent picture, the reality of voice, and the searching penetration of the novel. I believe Mr. Preston Sturges is the first author to avail himself of the full resources of the new medium. It is a pleasure and a privilege to present this powerful story to the American public."

. . . Spencer Tracy, Colleen Moore, and the makeup department have a field day skipping about through the years. In other words, "narratage" turns out to be the time-honored flashback, burdened with the mannerisms of a modern radio announcer.

James Shelley Hamilton,
National Board of Review magazine

The Power and the Glory has a good deal of sincerity in its acting and excellent direction to recommend it. Some of its press-agent ballyhoo borders on absurdity: its salesmen have claimed for it a new cinema technique, and have even put a bronze tablet in a New York theatre commemorating the first public showing of "the first motion picture in which narratage was used as a method of telling a dramatic story." That slightly illegitimate word "narratage," thought up by some eager mind in imitation of montage, means only an off-screen voice helping to tell the story, with comments. Far from being a novelty, it was tried most unhappily in the first American version of *White Hell of Pitz Palu* (1930), in which the excitable Graham McNamee ranted so vigorously that audiences rebelled and stayed away, and another version *sans narratage*—far more effective—was resurrected. This style of narrative-comment is probably most familiar in *Screen Souvenirs* and their various imitations. However, whether novel or not, the method adds little but confusion to *The Power and the Glory,* and of course adds nothing to cinematic technique: quite the contrary. The plot of the picture, concerned with the career of a railroad magnate to whom success brought unhappiness and a turgid triangular tragedy involving his son and his second wife, owes a tremendous debt to such actors as Colleen Moore and Spencer Tracy and to the sympathetic skill of William K. Howard as director.

With Claire Trevor

The Mad Game

1933

Produced and distributed by Fox. A Sol Wurtzel Production. Director: Irving Cummings. Original story and screenplay by William Conselman and Henry Johnson.

Photography: Arthur Miller. Musical Director: Samuel Kaylin. Recording Engineer: S. C. Chapman. Release date: October 27, 1933. Running time: 73 minutes.

The Cast

Edward Carson	Spencer Tracy
Jane Lee	Claire Trevor
Judge Penfield	Ralph Morgan
Thomas Penfield	Harold Lolly
Lila Penfield	Mary Mason
Chopper Allen	J. Carrol Naish
William Bennett	John Miljan

and Matt McHugh, Kathleen Burke, Willard Robertson, John Davidson, Paul Fix, and Jerry Devine

Synopsis

Ed Carson, head of a bootlegging mob, is framed by his lawyer and sent to prison for income tax evasion. Meanwhile his gang turns from selling liquor, now that its sale has been legalized, to the kidnapping racket. Thomas and Lila Penfield, son and daughter-in-law of Judge Penfield, who sent Carson to prison, are kidnapped by the gang. Carson is paroled to help capture the kidnappers and rescue the Penfields. Carson finds Tom and Lila, sets them free, and kills the leader of the kidnappers, but is himself fatally wounded.

With Claire Trevor

A Man's Castle

1933

Produced and distributed by Columbia. Director: Frank Borzage. Assistant Director: Lew Borzage. Screenplay by Jo Swerling, based on a play by Lawrence Hazard.

Photography: Joseph August. Editor: Viola Lawrence. Recording Engineer: Wilbur Brown. Release date: November 4, 1933. Running time: 75 minutes.

With Loretta Young

With Loretta Young and Walter Connelly

With Loretta Young

With Loretta Young

*With Marjorie Rambeau
and Arthur Hohl*

With Helen Mackellar (whose role was taken over by Marjorie Rambeau midway through the making of the film), Walter Connelly, and Loretta Young.

The Cast

Bill	Spencer Tracy
Trina	Loretta Young
Fay LaRue	Glenda Farrell
Ira	Walter Connolly
Bragg	Arthur Hohl
Flossie	Marjorie Rambeau

and Dickie Moore, Helen Eddy, Harvey Clark, Robert Grey, Tony Merlo, Kendall McComas, Harry Watson, and Henry Roquemore

Synopsis

Bill, who lives in a Depression camp, finds Trina, hungry and desperate, and takes her to live with him in his hovel. Bill works at various odd jobs to keep himself going. But when he meets a showgirl who will support him, he realizes he has it made. Then he discovers that Trina is going to have a baby, so he leaves Fay LaRue, the showgirl, returns to Trina and marries her. Bill and a friend attempt to rob a factory office safe, but fail. Trina and Bill leave the camp, and hop a freight to find another place where they can make a new start in life.

An "on the set" shot, with Spencer Tracy and Arthur Hohl. Seated and watching them is director Frank Borzage. At the camera is Joseph August.

With Jack Oakie

With Constance Cummings

Looking for Trouble

1934

Produced by Twentieth Century. Distributed by United Artists. A Darryl F. Zanuck Production. Associate Producers: William Goetz and Raymond Griffith. Director: William Wellman. Screenplay by Leonard Praskins and Elmer Harris, based on an original story by J. R. Bren.

Photography: James Van Trees, Sr. Editor: Peter Fritch. Musical Director: Alfred Newman. Art Directors: Richard Day and Joseph Wright. Release date: March 9, 1934. Running time: 80 minutes.

With Jack Oakie

With Judith Wood

With Constance Cummings

The Cast

Joe Graham	Spencer Tracy	Pearl	Judith Wood
Casey	Jack Oakie	Dan	Morgan Conway
Ethel	Constance Cummings	Regan	Paul Harvey
Maizie	Arline Judge	Max	Joseph Sauers
		Martin	Franklin Ardell

With Robert Homans, Constance Cummings, and Arlene Judge

105

From the Long Beach earthquake sequence, with Judith Wood and Jack Oakie

Synopsis

Joe, an ace trouble-shooter for the telephone company, is teamed with Casey. Although very much in love with Ethel, Joe continually quarrels with her. In an attempt to prove Ethel's boss, Dan, is a crook, both Joe and Casey are trapped by some criminals and left to die in a burning building. Joe sets off the fire alarm, saves Casey's life, and helps capture the criminals. Later, Dan is found dead and Ethel is a prime suspect. After much trouble, Joe finds Pearl, an old friend of Dan's, who makes a last-minute confession exonerating Ethel of any guilt.

With Arlene Judge, Jack Oakie, and Constance Cummings

106

With Madge Evans

The Show-Off

1934

Produced and distributed by Metro-Goldwyn-Mayer. Produced by Lucien Hubbard. Directed by Charles F. Riesner. Screenplay by Herman J. Mankiewicz, based on the play by George Kelly. Photography: James Wong Howe. Editor: William S. Gray. Art Director: David Townsend. Sound Director: Douglas Shearer. Release date: March 23, 1934. Running time: 79 minutes.

The Cast

Aubrey Piper	Spencer Tracy
Amy Fisher	Madge Evans
Clara	Lois Wilson
Pa Fisher	Grant Mitchell
Ma Fisher	Clara Blandick
J. B. Preston	Claude Gillingwater
Joe	Henry Wadsworth
Frank	Alan Edward
Edwards	Richard Tucker

Synopsis

Aubrey Piper, although only a clerk, pretends to be a railroad mogul and wins Amy Fisher's affections. He does not, however, fool Ma Fisher. Going too far, Aubrey cannot fulfill his promises, loses his job, and is thrown out of the Fisher home. He ends up wearing an advertising sandwich board, the only job he can get. He meets Joe, who has a patent, and helps him sell it for a high price. Then a deal that Aubrey worked out for the railroad succeeds. Back on top, he gets the impressionable Amy to marry him. Then he begins to develop new schemes as Ma Fisher looks on, wondering what new foolishness she will have to endure.

Review

Newsweek

Spencer Tracy has never given a bad screen performance. In the title role of this MGM comedy of family life he gives one of his best.

It is a filming of George Kelly's play, which had nearly 600 performances on Broadway in 1927–8, with the late Louis Bartels in the lead. Both the screening and Tracy's acting compare favorably with the originals.

Herbert Mundin, Pat Patterson,
and Sid Silvers

Bottoms Up

1934

Produced and distributed by Fox. Produced by B. G. DeSylva. Directed by David Butler. Original story and screenplay by B. G. DeSylva, David Butler, and Sid Silvers. Photography: Arthur Miller. Editor: Irene Marra. Musical Director: C. Bakaleinikoff. Orchestral arrangements: Howard Jackson. Music and lyrics by Harold Adamson, Burton Lane, Richard Whiting, and Gus Kahn. Dance Director: H. Hecht. Art Director: Gordon Wiles. Dance sets by Russell Patterson. Costumes: Russell Patterson. Sound Engineer: Joseph Aiken. Release date: April 13, 1934. Running time: 85 minutes.

With Herbert Mundin and Sid Silvers

The Cast

Smoothe King	Spencer Tracy
Hal Reed	John Boles
Wanda Gale	Pat Patterson
Limey Brook	Herbert Mundin
Spud Mosco	Sid Silvers
Louis Baer	Harry Green
Judith Marlowe	Thelma Todd
Detective Rooney	Robert Emmett O'Connor
Lane Worthing	Del Henderson
Secretary	Susanne Kaaren
Baldwin	Douglas Wood

Synopsis

Smoothe King, a slick promoter, disguises his forger pal and Wanda Gale, an extra, as a pair of British nobility, and helps them crash the gate of a movie company. As Wanda becomes a star, King sees her falling in love with the screen idol instead of himself. When the final crisis comes, he sacrifices his own hopes to the girl's happiness and success, and seeks new suckers to trim.

With Helen Twelvetrees

Now I'll Tell

1934

Distributed by Fox. A Winfield Sheehan Production. Director: Edwin Burke. Screenplay by Edwin Burke, based on the book by Mrs. Arnold Rothstein. Photography: Ernest Palmer. Musical Director: Arthur Lange. Musical score: Hugo Friedhofer, Arthur Lange, and David Buttolph. Art Director: Jack Otterson. Sound Engineer: William D. Flick. Release date: June 8, 1934. Running time: 72 minutes.

With Hobart Cavanaugh and
Alice Faye

The Cast

Murray Golden	Spencer Tracy
Virginia	Helen Twelvetrees
Peggy	Alice Faye
Mossiter	Robert Gleckler
Freddie	Hobart Cavanaugh
Doran	Henry O'Neill
Hart	G. P. Huntley, Jr.
Mary Doran	Shirley Temple

and Ronnie Cosbey, Ray Cooke, Frank Marlowe, Clarence Wilson, Barbara Weeks, Theodore Newton, Jr., Vince Barnett, and Jim Donlon

Synopsis

A small-time gambler, Murray Golden, uses Blue Book names to gain prestige. He promises his wife, Virginia, who never associates with his activities, to quit when he has made $200,000. He fixes a fight, only to gain the enmity of Mossiter, a gang leader. A mix-up with Peggy, who is subsequently killed in an auto accident, angers his wife, who leaves him. Golden finally loses his fortune to Mossiter. Pawning his wife's jewels, Golden buys an insurance policy and goes to meet his doom, leaving the insurance money to his wife.

With Hobart Cavanaugh

With Ronnie Cosbey and Shirley Temple

Review

Argus, *The Literary Digest*

Ostensibly woven out of the sensational career and violent death of one of New York's most notorious gamblers, the film belies its sensational title. At the hands of Edwin Burke, adapter, director, and dialog-writer of the offering, it becomes a sharply outlined

With Alice Faye

and colorful portrait of a man obsessed with a desire for power through money and achieving that end by gambling on anything from the flip of a coin to a crooked prizefight. As a biography of Arnold Roth-stein, it leaves much to be desired, but as a picture of the fringe of a big metropolis' underworld it is an effective and exciting melodrama.

Spencer Tracy does one of his finest jobs of acting in the film, keeping the central character both credible and in a measure sympathetic.

With Ketti Gallian

With Ketti Gallian

Marie Galante

1934

Produced and distributed by Fox. A Winfield Sheehan Production. Director: Henry King. Screenplay by Reginald Berkeley, based on a novel by Jacques Deval. Photography: John Seitz. Musical Director: Arthur Lange. Release date: October 26, 1934. Running time: 88 minutes.

The Cast

Crawbett	Spencer Tracy
Marie Galante	Ketti Gallian
Plosser	Ned Sparks
Tapia	Helen Morgan
Brogard	Siegfried Rumann
Tanoki	Leslie Fenton
General Phillips	Arthur Byron
Ratcliff	Robert Lorraine
Sailor	Jay C. Flippen
Ellsworth	Frank Darien
Bartender	Stepin Fetchit

Synopsis

Marie Galante is kidnapped by a drunken sea captain, who claims she is a stowaway and throws her off the ship at Yucatán. She makes her way to the Panama Canal zone, where she earns money singing in a café. She becomes involved in a counterspy plot to sabotage the Canal. Crawbett, the American intelligence officer, believes her kidnapping story, attempts to help her, and then falls in love with her. The plot is uncovered, and the Canal is saved.

With Ketti Gallian

With Wendy Barrie and Raymond Walburn

It's a Small World

1935

Produced and distributed by Fox. Producer: Edward Butcher. Director: Irving Cummings. Screenplay by Samuel Hellman and Gladys Lehman, based on Highway Robbery *by Albert Treynor. Photography: Arthur Miller. Score and Musical Direction: Arthur Lange. Art Director: William Darling. Sound Engineer: S. C. Chapman. Release date: April 12, 1935. Running time: 70 minutes.*

With Wendy Barrie and Raymond Walburn

With Wendy Barrie

The Cast

Bill Shevlin	Spencer Tracy
Jane Dale	Wendy Barrie
Judge Julius B. Clummerhorn	Raymond Walburn
Lizzie	Virginia Sale
Nancy Naylor	Astrid Allwyn
Cal	Irving Bacon
Cyclone	Charles Seldon
Motor Cop	Nick Foran
Mrs. Dale	Belle Daube
Snake Brown, Jr.	Frank McGlynn, Sr.
Snake Brown III	Frank McGlynn, Jr.
Snake Brown, Sr.	Bill Gillis
Buck Bogardus	Edwin Brady
Freddie Thompson	Harold Minjir

Synopsis

Miss Jane Dale, a socialite, and Bill Shevlin, a young lawyer, meet in an auto accident in a small southern town. Julius B. Clummerhorn, who is judge, sheriff, taxi driver, barber, game warden, hotel and garage owner, arrests the two and decides to hold a trial. As the trial, burdened with ridiculous interruptions, progresses, Shevlin falls in love with Miss Dale. She decides to be difficult until Shevlin proves his ability as a dog-trainer and then she realizes how much she loves him.

With Virginia Bruce

Murder Man

1935

Produced and distributed by Metro-Goldwyn-Mayer. Producer: Harry Rapf. Director: Tim Whelan. Assistant Director: David Friedman. Screenplay by Tim Whelan and John C. Higgins, based on a story by Tim Whelan and Guy Bolton. Photography: Lester White. Editor: James E. Newcomb. Musical score by William Axt. Art Director: Cedric Gibbons. Associate Art Directors: Eddie Imazu and Edwin B. Willis. Sound Director: Douglas Shearer. Release date: July 12, 1935. Running time: 70 minutes.

The Cast

Steve Gray	Spencer Tracy
Mary Shannon	Virginia Bruce
Captain Cole	Lionel Atwell
Henry Mander	Harvey Stephens
Robins	Robert Barrat
Shorty	James Stewart
Pop Gray	William Collier, Sr.
Carey Booth	Bobby Watson
Red Maquire	William Demarest

and John Sheehan, Lucien Littlefield, George Chandler, Fuzzy Knight, Louise Henry, Robert Warwick, Joe Irving, and Ralph Bushman

Synopsis

Steve Gray, a newspaper reporter, takes revenge on two criminals for victimizing his father and causing his wife's suicide. He places the blame for his own killing on one of them, Henry Mander. Shortly before Mander is to be executed, Gray visits him in prison for a final interview, but then confesses his guilt and accepts the punishment.

Review

Time

. . . *The Murder Man* is consequently only a little better than the average pop-gun and city-room mystery play, distinguished mainly by the agreeable acting of its two seasoned principals, Spencer Tracy and Virginia Bruce.

*With Lionel Atwill, John Sheehan,
and Lucien Littlefield*

With Virginia Bruce

117

Dante's Inferno

1935

Produced and distributed by Fox. Producer: Sol M. Wurtzel. Director: Harry Lachman. Screenplay by Philip Klein and Robert M. Yost. Photography: Rudolph Mate. Editor: Al DeGaetano. Musical score by Hugo Friedhofer, Samuel Kaylin, R. H. Bassett, and Peter Brunelli. Musical Director: Samuel Kaylin. Allegorical sets designed by Willy Pogany. Release date: August 30, 1935. Running time: 88 minutes.

The Cast

Jim Carter	Spencer Tracy
Betty McWade	Claire Trevor
Pop McWade	Henry B. Walthall
Jonesy	Alan Dinehart
Alexander Carter	Scott Beckett
Dean	Robert Gleckler
Inspector Harris	Willard Robertson
Captain Morgan	Morgan Wallace
Dancers	Rita Cansino and Gary Leon

With Claire Trevor and Henry B. Walthall

With Henry B. Walthall and Claire Trevor

With Claire Trevor

With Henry B. Walthall

With Henry B. Walthall

Synopsis

Jim Carter, a stoker aboard a ship, is fired. He wanders about, arriving on a carnival midway where he meets McWade and his niece, Betty, who run a concession in which are re-created scenes from Dante's *Inferno* for the moral edification of the customers. Carter revolutionizes the barking methods and puts the "Inferno" on a paying basis, but in doing so, he causes the suicide of a man who stood in his way. His attentions are given to gaining more power and money, although he doesn't lose his affection for Betty, whom he has now married, and their son. The amusement pier is called unsafe by an inspector, but Carter bribes him to overlook the matter. The place crashes, and the inspector kills himself. Pop McWade is also injured in the accident, and from his sickbed recounts several of the moral tales from Dante's poem. On trial, Carter denies the bribe, and his wife's testimony saves him. But considering their happiness ruined by his conduct, she leaves him, taking their son with her. Carter then puts all his money into a floating gambling palace, and to avoid a delay caused by a strike, he hires an inexperienced crew. Carter's son is brought to visit him on the boat. A fire breaks out, the crew deserts, but Carter is able to beach the boat, saving the lives of those on board. He has lost his fortune but learned his lesson. A reconciliation with Betty follows and they look hopefully forward to a new future.

With Myrna Loy

Whipsaw

1935

Produced and distributed by Metro-Goldwyn-Mayer. Producer: Harry Rapf. Director: Sam Wood. Assistant Director: Eddie Woehler. Screenplay by Howard E. Rogers, based on a story by James E. Grant. Photography: James Wong Howe. Editor: Basil Wrangell. Musical score by William Axt. Art Director: Cedric Gibbons. Associate Art Directors: William Horning and Edwin B. Willis. Wardrobe by Dolly Tree. Sound Director: Douglas Shearer. Release date: December 6, 1935. Running time: 83 minutes.

The Cast

Vivian Palmer	Myrna Loy
Ross McBride	Spencer Tracy
Ed Dexter	Harvey Stephens
Doc Evans	William Harrigan
Harry Ames	Clay Clement
Steve Arnold	Robert Gleckler
Wadsworth	Robert Warwick

and Halliwell Hobbes, Paul Stanton, Wade Boteler, Don Rowan, John Qualen, Irene Franklin, Lillian Leighton, J. Anthony Hughes, William Ingersoll, Charles Irwin, and George Renevent

With Myrna Loy

*With Myrna Loy, William Inger-
soll, and John Qualen*

Synopsis

Vivian Palmer, Dexter, and Ames steal valuable jewels in Paris. Rival gangsters Evans and Arnold take the loot away from them. However, Dexter and Ames get the jewelry back when both gangs arrive in New York. McBride, a G-man in disguise, joins Miss Palmer as she travels across the country with the jewels. She falls in love with him, quits the gang; but he finds the jewelry and arrests her. Both gangs arrive on the scene and there is a big gun fight. McBride is wounded, but victorious. Miss Palmer is cleared and remains with McBride as the remaining gangsters are taken away.

Review

Time

[Not an important film], but Myrna Loy's charm and Tracy's skillful underplaying are assets that no picture can have and be bad.

With Myrna Loy

With Jean Harlow, Una Merkel, and Mickey Rooney

Riffraff

1936

Produced and distributed by Metro-Goldwyn-Mayer. Producer: Irving Thalberg. Associate Producer: David Lewis. Director: J. Walter Ruben. Assistant Director: Dolph Zimmer. Screenplay by Frances Marion, H. W. Hanemann, and Anita Loos, based on an original story by Frances Marion. Photography: Ray June. Editor: Frank Sullivan. Musical score by Edward Ward. Art Director: Cedric Gibbons. Associate Art Director: Stanwood Rogers. Wardrobe by Dolly Tree. Sound Recording Director: Douglas Shearer. Release date: January 3, 1936. Running time: 89 minutes.

The Cast

Hattie	Jean Harlow
Dutch	Spencer Tracy
Lil	Una Merkel
Nick	Joseph Calleia
"Flytrap"	Victor Kilian
Jimmy	Mickey Rooney

and J. Farrell MacDonald, Roger Imhof, Juanita Quigley, Paul Hurst, Vince Barnett, Dorothy Appleby, Judith Wood, Arthur Housman, Wade Boteler, Joe Phillips, William Newell, Al Hill, Helen Flint, Lillian Harmer, Bob Perry, George Givot, Helene Costello, and Rafaelo Ottiano

Synopsis

Dutch, a fisherman, marries Hattie, who works in the cannery. Because he helped settle a strike, Dutch has funny ideas of his own importance, and manages to get his mates into trouble. For this he is expelled from the union and fired from his job. He deserts Hattie and goes away. Hearing he needs money, she steals for him, is caught and sent to prison. A friend gets Dutch a new job at which he frustrates a plot to dynamite the ship, and so becomes the hero of the day. Hattie escapes from prison, but is caught again, but before she goes back, she asks Dutch to wait for her, which he promises to do.

123

With Jean Harlow

Review

Hollywood Spectator

David Lewis, producer in charge of *Riffraff,* does with it what David Selznick did with *Tale of Two Cities.* He makes a giant of the production and a dwarf of the story. There are so many crowds milling through the picture, so much uproar and confusion, it is difficult at times to distinguish between story and superfluous production. A producer should know a screen story cannot be written with hammers and saws, nor can scenes gain strength from the bulk of their physical contents. A man, alone on a raft at sea, spying a shred of smoke rising on the horizon, can be more dramatic than the pounding feet of ten thousand soldiers marching through a picture at the expense of the story.

A picture succeeds as entertainment only to the extent it interests us in the fate of the individuals. The ten thousand soldiers can serve as an impressive background to the drummer boy marching at their head, if it is he we are interested in, but they have no story value on their own account. *Riffraff* shows us so many people so many times we lose sight of individuals and cannot sustain uninterruptedly our interest in them. Nor can we measure the value of a story by the noise it makes in its telling.

The characters in *Riffraff* howl at one another in scenes that would be more convincing if the dialogue were spoken softly. It is the intonation of voices, not their volume of sound, that makes them impressive. Nor is it the volume alone which makes loud dialogue irritating; it is our nearness to the characters in close shots and our consciousness that we could hear them if they whispered.

Walter Ruben, the director, might argue that he was dealing with rough waterfront characters with nerves strong enough to withstand the vocal assaults. I granted him that much for the greater part of the footage, but when Jean Harlow and Spencer Tracy yelled at one another in a scene which could have been made convincing only by subdued dialogue, I realized that he was revelling in uproar on its own account. Jean is being sought by officers after her escape from prison. Tracy encounters her in a waterfront home which is little more than a shack. Police are watching the place.

To sustain the drama inherent in the situation, it was essential they should converse in whispers. Instead, they shout at one another at the tops of their voices. Thus it was not the fact of their shouting in itself which ruined the scene; it was the assininity of the two characters for whose misfortunes our sympathies must be engaged if the story is to mean anything to us. And the shouting in this scene made me ascribe all that had preceded it to inefficient direction.

The story is an involved one. Jean Harlow is provided with more relatives than we can keep track of handily. Sociological problems are suggested but not solved. Jean tries hard but never gained my entire sympathy. I am a sentimental old duffer, with tears ready to gush in response to the slightest provocation, but I was unmoved when Jean's baby was taken from her in jail. It was not Jean's fault. I have great admiration for her acting ability, but this time the odds against her were too great.

Spencer Tracy is a bumptious, conceited ass throughout, giving a really splendid delineation of the character handed him, but it is not one that audiences will warm to. We do not go to pictures to be entertained by acting. We go to have stories told us by people who do not suggest they are acting. The very fact of its being obvious throughout that Jean and Tracy were acting makes their performances unconvincing.

Several members of the too-long cast meet the necessary requirements. Una Merkel and J. Farrell MacDonald are entirely human and likeable. With her every appearance, Una is making herself more valuable to the screen. She is intelligent, adaptable, and has a lively sense of humor. MacDonald is a great asset to any picture in which he is given an opportunity to develop his strong human quality. Joseph Calleia is another of the few quietly speaking, non-irritating members of the cast, his lack of histrionic exuberance marking him as an excellent actor. Vince Barnett strikes a sympathetic note.

Metro mounted the picture in the meritorious manner characteristic of all its productions, and Ray June photographed it with rare skill. The story, an original by Frances Marion, must have become involved after it left her hands, for she long ago contracted the habit of turning out only excellent story material.

I do not intend to convey the impression that *Riffraff* is entirely without merit. I would recommend it to you as screen entertainment you should see. Its fishing industry background is virile, picturesque relief from drawing rooms and boudoirs, and if you happen to be less susceptible to noise than I am, you may find the story more interesting than I did.

With Ernie Alexander

Fury

1936

Produced and distributed by Metro-Goldwyn-Mayer. Producer: Joseph L. Mankiewicz. Director: Fritz Lang. Assistant Director: Horace Hough. Screenplay by Bartlett Cormack and Fritz Lang, based on an original story by Norman Krasna. Photography: Joseph Ruttenberg. Editor: Frank Sullivan. Musical score by Franz Waxman. Art Director: Cedric Gibbons. Associate Art Directors: William A. Horning and Edwin B. Willis. Wardrobe by Dolly Tree. Recording Director: Douglas Shearer. Release date: May 29, 1936. Running time: 90 minutes.

The Cast

Katherine Grant	Sylvia Sydney
Joe Wilson	Spencer Tracy
District Attorney	Walter Abel
Kirby Dawson	Bruce Cabot
Sheriff	Edward Ellis
Bugs Meyers	Waltre Brennan
Tom	George Walcott
Charlie	Frank Albertson
Durkin	Arthur Stone
Fred Garrett	Morgan Wallace
Milton Jackson	George Chandler
Stranger	Roger Gray
Vickery	Edwin Maxwell
Governor	Howard Hickman
Defense Attorney	Jonathan Hale
Edna Hooper	Leila Bennett
Mrs. Whipple	Esther Dale
Franchette	Helen Flint

With Sylvia Sidney

126

*With Frank Albertson and
George Walcott*

Synopsis

Joe Wilson, a young man, is on his way to meet the girl he plans to marry. Passing through a small town where there has been a kidnapping, he is picked up and jailed as a suspect. The citizens form a lynch mob, attack the jail, and burn it down. This is recorded by newsreel cameras. The suspected kidnapper [Joe] is believed killed. But he has escaped, and is in hiding. He summons his brothers, tells them to get the film as proof and arrest the members of the mob so they can be tried for his murder. The trial is held and the film identification makes conviction almost certain. His brothers beg him to reveal himself—the mob was not guilty of his murder—but Joe wants revenge. Finally, his sweetheart is able to soften his heart and he appears in court. The case against the mob members is dismissed.

Sylvia Sidney

Reviews

Literary Digest

From Metro-Goldwyn-Mayer, which appears to be treating itself to a sackful of excellent motion pictures, comes *Fury,* a grim, sometimes terrifying film document showing the ferocity of mob-rule. From an original story by Norman Krasna, Bartlett Cormack and the picture's director, Fritz Lang, have made a scenario of stunning vigor. It will, in some parts of the country, be recognized as a sobering force.

... That many of its situations are trite is not to be denied. That Director Lang has passed these with skill gives the picture strength where it might have been weak.

Spencer Tracy brings lasting reality to the role of Joe, victim of the mob, and has sturdy support from Sylvia Sidney, Walter Abel, and Bruce Cabot.

Robert Giroux, *The Nation*

How to disturb an audience is of course as big a problem in the cinema as in the theater. Director Fritz Lang has been highly successful with the problem in his first American movie, made after more than a year of idleness in Hollywood. One might say too successful, for *Fury* is disturbing for the wrong reason: the problem it poses is entirely unresolved at the close. The audience is subjected to a high degree of strain during the cumulative course of the film, but one's emotions are unpurged at the end, for the catharsis is incomplete. Mr. Lang and his associates have disregarded an important corollary to disturbing an audience, that is, calming it by fulfilling its aroused expectations.

There is no misunderstanding the abhorrence with which the makers of *Fury* regard lynching. The directorial presentation of the good citizens of Strand, U.S.A., burning the jail from which they cannot snatch Joe Wilson is quite clear; to make it even clearer Mr. Lang anatomizes every horrible detail of the mob in the newsreel shots used at the trial. But *Fury* is the story of Joe Wilson, and it is also clear that his vow, after his escape, to have the lynchers destroyed by the machinery of legal justice is a bitter and tragic one, for it means his self-destruction. At this point the film is already complete as tragedy. Joe Wilson has been changed from a sentimental and good-natured average man into an incurable victim of inhumanity; we await the resolution.

This is the meaning of the lynching—not merely that human beings are capable of acting like beasts, but that the lives of two people we know, Joe and his girl, and the lives of twenty-two citizens are ruined by it. The story by Norman Krasna seemed to be a perfect invention for saying this. What are we to understand, then, when Joe Wilson enters the court just as the death sentences are being pronounced and saves his lynchers? That one man was capable of an act of perfect charity? But Wilson curses his lynchers in court and vows he'll never be the same again, although he has just performed the one act impossible to his altered character. What does *Fury* mean? Nobody's hurt; Joe and his girl are ready to marry and start life over, and the lynchers have had a big scare. The whole business is, I suppose, just one of those messes which human beings are always getting in and out of.

In directing the film Mr. Lang makes full and efficient use of his imagination only in presenting the mob and in creating small-town life. It is regrettable that he did not, or could not, make *Fury* the first-rate tragedy it might have been. Spencer Tracy and Sylvia Sidney are handicapped by dull opening scenes, but their acting improves as the film gains in intensity.

128

San Francisco

1936

Produced and distributed by Metro-Goldwyn-Mayer. A W. S. Van Dyke Production. Producers: John Emerson and Bernard H. Hyman. Director: W. S. Van Dyke. Assistant Director: Joseph Newman. Screenplay by Anita Loos, based on a story by Robert Hopkins. Photography: Oliver T. Marsh. Editor: Tom Held. Montage sequences: John Hoffman. Musical Director: Herbert Stothart. Musical score: Edward Ward. Song: "San Francisco" by Gus Kahn, B. Kaper, and W. Jurmann. Song: "Would You" by Nacio Brown and Arthur Freed. Art Director: Cedric Gibbons. Associate Art Directors: Arnold Gillespie, Harry McAfee, and Edwin B. Willis. Gowns by Adrian. Recording Director: Douglas Shearer. Dances staged by Val Raset. Operatic sequences staged by William von Wymetal. Release date: June 26, 1936. Running time: 115 minutes.

The Cast

Blackie Norton	Clark Gable
Mary Blake	Jeanette MacDonald
Father Mullin	Spencer Tracy
Jack Burley	Jack Holt
Mrs. Burley	Jessie Ralph
Mat	Ted Healy
Trixie	Shirley Ross
Della Bailey	Margaret Irving
Babe	Harold Huber
Professor	Al Shean
Signor Baldini	William Ricciardi
Chick	Kenneth Harlan
Alaska	Roger Imhof
Tony	Charles Judells
Red Kelly	Russell Simpson
Freddie Duane	Bert Roach
Hazeltine	Warren B. Hymer
Sheriff	Edgar Kennedy

With Clark Gable

With Jeanette MacDonald

Synopsis

Mary Blake comes to San Francisco, ambitious for an operatic career, but circumstances force her to accept an entertainer's position in Blackie Norton's Barbary Coast café. Grateful to Blackie for his help, but afraid of his intentions, she finds confidence in the counsel of Father Mullin, an old friend of Blackie's. An aristocrat, Jack Burley, hears her singing and offers to help her develop her career. Blackie and Burley, now rivals, determine to destroy each other. The love of Mary will be the reward for the victor. Then Mary discovers that Burley's intentions are not honorable. She enters a contest and wins the first prize, which she offers to Blackie to help him. Because of stubborn pride he rejects the prize money—and Mary. A horrendous earthquake destroys the city. Blackie, realizing his love for Mary, searches for her, and finds her with Father Mullin, ministering to the injured and the dying. Blackie is thankful that Mary's life has been spared.

Review

Frank S. Nugent, *The New York Times*

Out of the gusty, brawling, catastrophic history of the Barbary Coast early in the century, Metro-Goldwyn-Mayer has fashioned a prodigally generous and completely satisfying screenplay. *San Francisco* is less a single motion picture than an anthology. During its two-hour course on the Capitol's screen it manages to encompass most of the virtues of the operatic film—the romantic, the biographical, the dramatic and the documentary. Astonishingly, it serves all of them abundantly well, truly meriting commendation as a near-perfect illustration of the cinema's inherent and acquired ability to absorb and digest other art forms and convert them into its own sinews.

Especially is this true of the picture's handling of the

entrancing musical sequences arranged for the lyric soprano voice of Jeanette MacDonald. Woven gracefully into the script, rather than patched over it to conceal gaps in the story fabric, they are an integral, as well as a delightful, part of the film. Seeking symbolism in the cinema is probably a thankless pursuit, yet one might present a defensible argument that Miss MacDonald's alternate indulgence in operatic arias and cabaret chantey was no less typical of the groping, immature spirit of wayward, flamboyant, young San Francisco than was Clark Gable's arrogant godlessness as the picture's Blackie Norton, or Jessie Ralph's proud independence in the role of one of the "old settlers" on Nob Hill.

Primarily, of course, this is the tale of a city, a vigorous story told in splashing melodramatic phrases and with the rich vocabulary of a thoroughly expert cast and one of the shrewdest directors in Hollywood, W. S. Van Dyke. It is the tale of San Francisco from New Year's Eve of 1906 until that early morning of April 18 of the same year when the earth convulsed and buildings fell and fire destroyed the city that had gained the reputation of being the wickedest on the Pacific Coast.

But one cannot reduce Mr. Gable, Miss MacDonald, Spencer Tracy, Jack Holt and the others in the cast to mere abstractions. *San Francisco* tells their story, too, and with a wealth of dramatic details that cannot be imprisoned in any brief synopsis.

The earthquake is a shattering spectacle, one of the truly great cinematic illusions; a monstrous, hideous, thrilling debacle with great fissures opening in the earth, buildings crumbling, men and women apparently being buried beneath showers of stone and plaster, gar-

With Clark Gable

130

goyles lurching from rooftops, watermains bursting, live wires flaring, flame, panic and terror.

For so impressive and thoroughly entertaining a picture, only a round robin of appreciation would do justice to the many who shared in its making.

. . . There must be special mention of another brilliant portrayal by Spencer Tracy, that of Father Mullin, the two-fisted chaplain of a Barbary Coast mission. Mr. Tracy, late of *Fury,* is headed surely toward an award for the finest performance of the year.

With Clark Gable and Jeanette MacDonald

With Clark Gable and Jeanette MacDonald

With Jean Harlow and
William Powell

Libeled Lady

1936

Produced and distributed by Metro-Goldwyn-Mayer. Producer: Lawrence Weingarten. Director: Jack Conway. Screenplay by Maurice Watkins, Howard Emmett Rogers, and George Oppenheimer, based on a story by Wallace Sullivan. Photography: Norbert Brodine. Editor: Frederick Y. Smith. Musical score by William Axt. Art Director: Cedric Gibbons. Associate Art Directors: William A. Horning and Edwin B. Willis. Wardrobe by Dolly Tree. Recording Director: Douglas Shearer. Release date: October 9, 1936. Running time: 98 minutes.

The Cast

Gladys	Jean Harlow
Bill Chandler	William Powell
Connie	Myrna Loy
Haggerty	Spencer Tracy

Mr. Allenbury	Walter Connolly
Mr. Bane	Charley Grapewin
Mrs. Burns-Norvell	Cora Witherspoon

and E. E. Clive, Lauri Beatty, Otto Yamoka, Charles Trowbridge, Spencer Charters, George Chandler, Greta Meyer, William Benedict, Hal K. Dawson, and William Newell

Synopsis

Newspaper editor Haggerty leaves his prospective bride, Gladys, at the church to determine why his paper printed a juicy scandal about millionairess Connie. Mr. Bane, the owner of the paper, has been plastered with a $5,000,000 libel suit because of the story. Haggerty searches the world over for Bill Chandler, expert lawyer, finds him on his own doorstep, and marries him to the amazed Gladys. Chandler goes to Europe and

With William Powell and
Jean Harlow

With Myrna Loy, William Powell, and Jean Harlow

worms his way into Connie's and her father's good graces. Chandler finds a compromising situation that will force withdrawal of the suit, but he falls in love with Connie and they elope. Then, clever lawyer that he is, Chandler proves his marriage to Gladys wasn't legal. Connie agrees to call off the suit. The problems solved, Haggerty marries Gladys.

Review

Frank S. Nugent, *The New York Times*

A libel suit can be a laughing matter, and *Libeled Lady* proves it. A sardonic comedy, with slapstick smudges and a liberal bedaubing of farce, it takes several freedoms with the press, liberties with the statutes, and jousts at justice—all in the merriest of moods. And offhand we can think of a dozen reasons why you should find it a thoroughly agreeable entertainment.

The first four reasons are obvious, being Jean Harlow, Myrna Loy, William Powell, and Spencer Tracy, who are just about as perfect a light-comedy foursome as you will encounter anywhere between the rockbound coast of Maine and the sun-kissed shores of California. The fifth would be Walter Connolly, who can register parental distraction with the best of them. The sixth is a zestful script, which has a generous spicing of witty lines and a fund of comic situations. The seventh is Jack Conway's agile direction. The eighth—but why be swamped with statistics? The assets are tangible enough without a detailed inventory.

With William Powell and
Jean Harlow

With Jean Harlow

With Franchot Tone

*With Gladys George and
Franchot Tone*

They Gave Him a Gun

1937

*Produced and distributed by Metro-Goldwyn-Mayer.
Producer: Harry Rapf. Director: W. S. Van Dyke. Assistant Director: Dolph Zimmer. Screenplay by Cyril
Hume, Richard Maibaum, and Maurice Rapf, based on
a book by William Joyce Cowen. Photography: Harold
Rosson. Editor: Ben Lewis. Montage and special effects: Slavko Vorkapich. Art Director: Cedric Gibbons.
Associate Art Directors: Harry McAfee and Edwin B.
Willis. Recording Director: Douglas Shearer. Release
date: May 14, 1937. Running time: 90 minutes.*

The Cast

Fred Willis	Spencer Tracy
Rose Duffy	Gladys George
Jimmy Davis	Franchot Tone
Sergeant Meadowlark	Edgar Dearing
Saxe	Mary Lou Treen
Laro	Cliff Edwards

and Charles Trowbridge, Joseph Sawyer, George
Chandler, Gavin Gordon, Ernest Whitman, Nita
Pike, and Joan Woodbury

Synopsis

Jimmy Davis, a weakling, is drafted and taught to use a gun. Fred Willis is in his troop; they become friends and are sent to Europe together. Fred falls in love with Rose, a nurse, but when he is reported missing, Jimmy quickly marries her. Jimmy uses his gun with extreme ferocity, becomes a hero, and receives a medal. Fred returns, is heartbroken by but accepts Jimmy's marriage to Rose.

Some years later, back in the States, Jimmy has become a gangster. When Rose discovers the truth, she stops Jimmy from participating in another gangland massacre by having him arrested. He goes to jail. Rose joins Fred's circus to have a job, but Jimmy thinks her unfaithful, escapes, and attempts to kill Fred, who takes his gun away and tells him he is a coward without it. Jimmy runs away and is shot by the police.

Reviews

Literary Digest

The cinema does not often pin on the wings of peace and flap them in eight reels of dove-like cooing. When it does, alas! it too frequently becomes so absorbed with the frantic didoes of war in the field that it loses grasp on its original message and whoops it up with sounds of thunder and scenes of carnage.

No sort of melodramatic side-tracking affects *They Gave Him a Gun*, a stark, super-realistic preachment against the evils of war as they apply to the individual. In it is some of the penetrative philosophy of the play *Johnny Johnson* and in it is an individual's-eyeview of war. It isn't pretty.

This is Producer Harry Rapf's testament that war not only is murder but teaches murder; that in the wake of war comes a regiment of young men suddenly thirsty to kill. No armistice, he implies, assuages that thirst and the soldiers carry it over into peace.

Metro turned three able players over to Rapf, tossed him a sum of money and asked him to do the job. It is not a job that is satisfactory in every respect; its story frequently stumbles around the middle of the road, but its general power is real and there are stunning performances by Spencer Tracy, Franchot Tone, and Miss Gladys George.

Tracy makes possibly the most emotionally right performance of his career in the role of the good fellow who isn't turned murderer by the killings of war. Tone uncovers depths hinted at in the theater five years ago, but not until now realized for the cinema. Miss George again proves that she is an emotional actress completely sure-footed, with a precision for powerful scenes that is astonishing.

Time

To balance its defects, *They Gave Him a Gun*, no masterpiece but a fast-moving, adult screenplay, has the advantage of highly proficient performances by its three principals.

With Franchot Tone

135

With Freddie Bartholomew

Captains Courageous

1937

Produced and distributed by Metro-Goldwyn-Mayer. Producer: Louis D. Lighton. Director: Victor Fleming. Marine Director: James Havens. Screenplay by John Lee Mahin, Marc Connelly, and Dale Van Every, based on the novel by Rudyard Kipling. Photography: Harold Rosson. Editor: Elmo Vernon. Musical score by Franz Waxman. Songs: music by Franz Waxman; lyrics by Gus Kahn. Art Director: Cedric Gibbons. Associate Art Directors: Arnold Gillispie and Edwin B. Willis. Recording Director: Douglas Shearer. Release date: June 25, 1937. Running time: 116 minutes.

With Freddie Bartholomew

*With Freddie Bartholomew and
Lionel Barrymore*

The Cast

Harvey Cheyne	Freddie Bartholomew	Cushman	Oscar O'Shea
Manuel	Spencer Tracy	Priest	Jack LaRue
Disko	Lionel Barrymore	Dr. Finley	Walter Kingsford
Mr. Cheyne	Melvyn Douglas	Tyler	Donald Briggs
Uncle Salters	Charles Grapewin	"Doc"	Samuel McDaniels
Dan	Mickey Rooney	Charles	Billy Burrud
"Long Jack"	John Carradine		

With Freddie Bartholomew

*With Freddie Bartholomew and
Lionel Barrymore*

*With Freddie Bartholomew and
John Carradine*

With Freddie Bartholomew

Synopsis

Harvey Cheyne is the pampered and yet neglected son of a business tycoon. The boy thinks he can make his way through life by lying, cheating, and crying. Thrown out of school, he travels to Europe with his father. Harvey falls off the liner as it passes the Grand Banks and is picked up by a fishing boat. While most of the crew find the boy too spoiled, Manuel, a Portuguese fisherman, takes care of the boy, who gradually succumbs to kindness he never knew before. During a race with another ship, Manuel falls into the sea and is killed. Harvey is heartbroken. The boat returns to Gloucester and Harvey is reunited with his father. Having learned some lessons of life, Harvey lights a candle in Manuel's memory.

Reviews

Time

. . . So magnificent are its sweep and excitement, so harmonious its design, that *Captains Courageous* ranks above most current cinematic efforts, offers its credentials for admission to the thin company of cinema immortals.

James Cunningham, *The Commonweal*

With no advance notice befitting its magnificence, Rudyard Kipling's immortalization of Gloucester's hardy and courageous fishing folk thrills us with fine seascapes and stirs us with the philosophy of the faith of a brawny though sentimental fisherman in the latent virtues hidden under the arrogance and selfishness of an obnoxiously spoiled son of a rich parent.

Freddie Bartholomew and Spencer Tracy are superb in their account of the evolution of the spoiled brat into a man, a lad who could only learn life's important lessons the hard way. Kipling kept life in his story, and so do its Hollywood narrators.

With Luise Rainer

With Luise Rainer, Paul Harvey, and William Demarest

Big City

1937

Produced and distributed by Metro-Goldwyn-Mayer. Producer: Norman Krasna. Director: Frank Borzage. Assistant Director: Lew Borzage. Screenplay by Dore Schary and Hugo Butler, based on an original story by Norman Krasna. Photography: Joseph Ruttenberg. Editor: Frederick Y. Smith. Musical score by William Axt. Art Director: Cedric Gibbons. Release date: September 3, 1937. Running time: 80 minutes.

The Cast

Joe Benton	Spencer Tracy
Anna Benton	Luise Rainer
The Mayor	Charley Grapewin
Sophie Sloane	Janet Beecher
Mike Edwards	Eddie Quillan
Paul Roya	Victor Varconi
John C. Andrews	Oscar O'Shea
Lola Johnson	Helen Troy

With Luise Rainer

With Luise Rainer

With Luise Rainer

and William Demarest, John Arledge, Irving Bacon, Guinn Williams, Regis Toomey, Edgar Dearing, Paul Harvey, Andrew J. Tombes, Clem Bevans, Grave Ford and Alice White; also, Jack Dempsey, James J. Jeffries, Jimmy McLarnin, Maxie Rosenbloom, Jim Thorp, Frank Wykoff, Jackie Fields, Man Mountain Dean, Gus Sonnenberg, George Godfrey, Joe Rivers, Cotton Warburton, Bull Montana, Snowy Baker, and Taski Hagio

Synopsis

In order to avert a taxi war the city officials decide to deport Anna Benton, wife of an independent taxi driver, placing responsibility on her for a recent bombing perpetrated by some gangsters. Joe Benton, her husband, learns what has happened just as her boat is about to sail. He appeals to the Mayor, who is addressing a banquet of veteran boxers. All those at the banquet go to the wharf, fight and capture the gangsters responsible for the trouble. Joe gets his wife off the boat just in time for her to have her baby in the ambulance.

With Joan Crawford and Alan Curtis

Mannequin

1938

Produced and distributed by Metro-Goldwyn-Mayer. Producer: Joseph L. Mankiewicz. Director: Frank Borzage. Assistant Director: Lew Borzage. Screenplay by Lawrence Hazard, based on an unpublished story by Katherine Brush. Photography: George Folsey. Editor: Frederick Y. Smith. Musical score by Edward Ward. Songs by Edward Ward, Robert Wright, and Chet Forrest. Art Director: Cedric Gibbons. Associate Art Directors: Paul Groesse and Edwin B. Willis. Costumes by Adrian. Recording Director: Douglas Shearer. Release date: January 28, 1938. Running time: 92 minutes.

The Cast

Jessie Cassidy	Joan Crawford
John Hennessey	Spencer Tracy
Eddie Miller	Alan Curtis
Briggs	Ralph Morgan
Beryl	Mary Phillips
Pa Cassidy	Oscar O'Shea
Mrs. Cassidy	Elizabeth Risdon
Clifford Cassidy	Leo Gorcey

and George Chandler, Bert Roach, Marie Blake, Matt McHugh, Paul Fix, Helen Troy, and Phillip Terry

With Joan Crawford

142

With Joan Crawford

Synopsis

John Hennessey, who came from Hester Street poverty to Park Avenue affluence, befriends two newly-weds from his old neighborhood. They are Jessie (Cassidy) and Eddie Miller. When Eddie's dishonest tendencies bring trouble and loss of money, he tells his wife that she must divorce him and marry Hennessey for his money, divorce him in turn and rejoin her former husband with Hennessey's money. She does divorce Eddie, but does not carry out his suggestion. Later she marries Hennessey with honorable intent; but when Eddie finds out, he threatens to tell Hennessey of the original scheme. However, Hennessey loses his fortune just in time to save his marriage.

With Joan Crawford

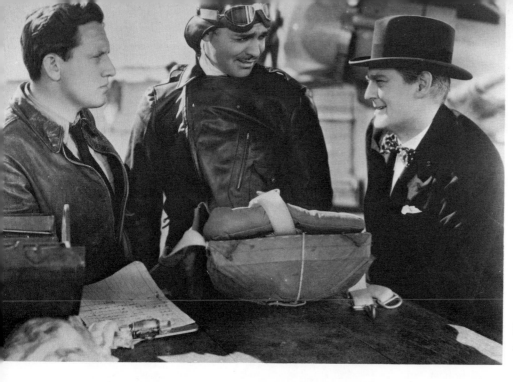

*With Clark Gable and
Lionel Barrymore*

Test Pilot

1938

Produced and distributed by Metro-Goldwyn-Mayer. Producer: Louis D. Lighton. Director: Victor Fleming. Screenplay by Vincent Lawrence and Waldemar Young, based on a story by Frank Wead. Photography: Ray June. Editor: Tom Held. Montage of Slavko Vorkapich. Musical score by Franz Waxman. Art Direction: Cedric Gibbons. Release date: April 22, 1938. Running time: 118 minutes.

The Cast

Jim	Clark Gable
Ann	Myrna Loy
Gunner	Spencer Tracy
Drake	Lionel Barrymore
General Ross	Samuel S. Hinds
Landlady	Marjorie Main
Joe	Ted Pearson
Mrs. Benson	Gloria Holden
Benson	Louis J. Heydt
Sarah	Virginia Grey
Mable	Priscilla Lawson
Mrs. Barton	Claudia Coleman
Mr. Barton	Arthur Aylesworth

Synopsis

Jim is a test pilot. It is a risky business with no future, hard on the body and nerves, sometimes driving the pilots to drink. Jim marries Ann, who gradually realizes the hazards of her husband's work. Both she and Gunner, Jim's buddy, try to keep Jim sober and sane. Finally Jim cracks up a plane, killing Gunner. This makes him decide to quit flying and take a ground job.

Article

Mark Van Doren, *The Nation*

The hero of *Test Pilot* is a loon (Clark Gable) who loves to risk his life by driving a pursuit plane or a bomber ballasted with sandbags to a height of six miles and then letting her drop. We see him pull on his padded suit and his oxygen tank; we follow him into the cockpit as another loon (Spencer Tracy) takes his gum out of his mouth and sticks it somewhere on the tail for good luck; we watch the plane lift itself with difficulty over trees and high-tension wires; we wallow upward with it to the dizzy place where instruments say it must begin to fall; and then we watch its long dive to earth—empty at the end perhaps because a wing has ripped off and Mr. Gable has had to descend separately under a parachute. Or there is the $10,000 race around pylons when our hero observes that his engine has caught fire and resolves nevertheless to finish the last sixteen miles; which he does, winning the ten grand and drinking half of it up that night—for this is a mad life, my masters, and one who leads it must either get drunk on such an occasion or say goodby to his nerves.

144

With Myrna Loy

Not to speak of the transcontinental speed trial which is interrupted over Kansas when an oil pump breaks down and Mr. Gable must descend to a grassy field over which comes running no less a farmer's daughter than Myrna Loy, who is engaged to a pleasant swain of the locality but decides within twenty-four hours to elope with Jim Lane and be married at Indianapolis. That, of course, is her initiation into loon life. She does not know yet, though she knows soon enough, what hell it is to be the wife of a man who is trying daily to kill himself. As she learns the lesson her nerves start to go, one by one, like the overstrained wires of a cable, snap, snap; and along with them go the nerves of Spencer Tracy, who shows it, however, only by knocking an occasional mechanic down or by folding himself into sudden silence while Clark and Myrna make eyes at each other or bandy bright words over champagne and highballs. Only in the last five minutes of a two-hour film, after Mr. Tracy is dead and Myrna has been reduced to maniacal fear, does Providence·in the shape of Mr. Gable's employer (Lionel Barrymore) step in and declare that henceforward he shall stay on the ground with a happy wife and a two-year-old son to help him take the final curtain.

If the tone of the above synopsis has seemed disrespectful, the reason is that something of the sort was

*With Myrna Loy and
Clark Gable*

With Clark Gable and Myrna Loy

necessary as a cover for the state of mind and body in which one spectator staggered forth from *Test Pilot*. Two hours of being on the stretch is a long time, and Metro-Goldwyn-Mayer have made few minutes of it merciful. It does no good to remember that many of the scenes in the sky were managed in miniature, with little tin planes turning through cotton clouds; or that the persons in whose lives we become interested are of course never off the ground; or that in the filming of the tale nobody actually died. *Test Pilot* as it stands—there is no use denying it—is a terrifying affair; and, since that is what it tried to be, it must be acknowl-

edged a success. That there are other ends at which to aim, that pity and terror can be perhaps more profitably felt when the heart is permitted to remain in its right place, that drama at its best is deeper than goose-flesh at its worse—these truths do not affect the fact that *Test Pilot* is on its peculiar level as incontrovertible as the explosion of ten planets. Personally I don't believe I can stand another sky thriller.

Time

. . . If a test pilot ends his career alive, he is considered lucky. *Test Pilot's* flying shots are among the best ever staged by cinema. But the picture is less concerned with the mechanics of test flying than it is with how test pilots and those about them live and act.

Its thoughtful story, by Lieut. Commander Frank Wead, conceives two sodden-nerved men, one a swaggering, hard-living and egotistic pilot (Gable), the other his patient, understanding mechanic (Tracy). On the fear-tortured mind of the flyer's wife (Myrna Loy) their almost brutal fatalism rasps like a file. Credit for blending this grounded mental conflict with the melodrama of wings in the air, screaming struts and whining motors goes to Director Victor Fleming. Not the least of his accomplishments was to exact performances that verge on reality from pert, actressy Myrna Loy and loud, slam-bang Clark Gable. From amenable, sandy Spencer Tracy, currently cinema's No. 1 actors' actor, Director Fleming got what he wanted without coaxing.

Newsweek

. . . Under Victor Fleming's direction, the performances of the three stars transform contrived emotion into the real thing. In fact, the film is just what Dr. Will Hays might have prescribed for the nation's ailing box offices.

Boys Town

1938

Distributed by Metro-Goldwyn-Mayer. Producer: John W. Considine, Jr. Director: Norman Taurog. Screenplay by John Meehan and Dore Schary, based on an *original story by Dore Schary and Eleanor Griffin. Photography: Sidney Wagner. Editor: Elmo Vernon. Special montage effects by Slavko Vorkapich. Musical score by Edward Ward. Musical arrangements by Leo Arnaud. Release date: September 9, 1938. Running time: 96 minutes.*

The Cast

Father E. Flanagan	Spencer Tracy
Whitey Marsh	Mickey Rooney
Dave Morris	Henry Hull
Dan Farrow	Leslie Fenton
The Judge	Addison Richards
Joe Marsh	Edward Norris
Tony Ponessa	Gene Reynolds
The Bishop	Minor Watson
The Sheriff	Victor Killian
John Hargraves	Jonathan Hale
Pee Wee	Bob Watson
Skinny	Martin Spellman
Tommy Anderson	Mickey Rentschler
Freddie Fuller	Frankie Thomas
Paul Ferguson	Jimmy Butler
Mo Kahn	Sidney Miller
Burton	Robert Keane

Synopsis

Father Flanagan hears a convict's bitter story which concludes with the idea that if he had been helped as a child, he might not have become a murderer. With the willing but skeptical help of pawnbroker Dave Morris, Father Flanagan creates the first poverty-stricken "Boys Town." The courts, the press, even the Bishop, at first doubt that he can succeed. But as the priest pleads and prays, the community grows. A thoroughly bad boy, Whitey Marsh, comes to live there. He sneers at the ideals. He tries to get his own way, but the other boys let him know he isn't the only one around. He runs away but comes back because he is hungry. Later, when he loses a fight, he runs away again, but returns when his friend Pee Wee is hit by an auto. Still, he is an outcast and so he runs away for a third time. This time he joins his brother, an escaped convict, and hides with him and his gang. A couple of boys find the hide-out and tell Father Flanagan, who returns with the boys and captures the criminals. The reward money saves "Boys Town."

With Bobs Watson

Review

Philip T. Hartung, *The Commonweal*

A burning desire to help his fellowmen and a belief that there is no such thing as a "bad boy" inspired and assisted the Reverend Edward J. Flanagan to found Boys Town. . . . Now Hollywood has seen fit to pay homage by tracing his story in a film. Metro-Goldwyn-Mayer should be thanked for their courage in making a picture that omits a love story, uses only men and boys for its leading characters and whose main plot concerns the fulfillment of a dream.

Spencer Tracy's sincere portrayal of the role of the priest is an outstanding work of his career, even better than his Father Tim in *San Francisco*. Without histrionics, Mr. Tracy simply *is* Father Flanagan in his efforts to raise money, in his taking in abandoned boys between the ages of twelve and eighteen, regardless of

With Frank Thomas, Mickey Rooney, and Sidney Miller

Newsweek

... Father Flanagan, sensitively portrayed by Spencer Tracy ...

Frank Nugent, *The New York Times*

It manages, in spite of the embarrassing sentimentality of its closing scenes, to be a consistently interesting and frequently touching motion picture. The Boys Town theme, with its firm basis in fact, is dramatic enough. Spencer Tracy's performance of Father Flanagan is perfection itself and the most eloquent tribute to the Nebraska priest.

Note

The Oscar won by Mr. Tracy for his portrayal of Father Flanagan, and given by him to Father Flanagan, occupies an honored position in a little museum we have at Boys Town. The inscription on the statuette reads: "Academy First Award to Spencer Tracy for his performance in *Boys Town*." The other inscription, added by Mr. Tracy, reads as follows: "To Father Edward J. Flanagan, whose great human qualities, kindly simplicity and inspiring courage were strong enough to shine through my humble efforts. S/Spencer Tracy."

Henry V. Straka
Director of Public Relations
Boys Town

race or creed, and in his fight to feed and teach and mother his friendless charges. It is unfortunate that the plain facts of Father Flanagan's history had to be interspersed with an overly sentimental drama of one of the boys' regeneration. Mickey Rooney runs the gamut of emotions from the tough, poker-playing gangster kid, through the tear-choked, made-over youngster, to the final noble youth who becomes mayor of Boys Town. But don't let this little sob story prevent your seeing *Boys Town*.

THE LIFE STORY OF A BOY WHO WAS "BORN TO BE HUNG"!

SPENCER TRACY
MICKEY ROONEY

"No boy is bad, if given a chance!"

M-G-M's THRILLING DRAMA!
BOYS TOWN

Screen play by
John Meehan and Dore Schary
Directed by
Norman Taurog
Produced by
John W. Considine Jr.

With Nancy Kelly

Stanley and Livingstone

1939

Produced and distributed by Twentieth Century–Fox. In charge of production: Darryl F. Zanuck. Associate Producer: Kenneth Macgowan. Director: Henry King. Assistant Director: Robert Webb. Screenplay by Philip Dunne and Julien Josephson, based on historical research and story outline by Hal Long and Sam Hellman. Photography: George Barnes. In charge of location shooting: Otto Brower. Guide and adviser for location shooting: Mrs. Osa Johnson. Editor: Barbara McLean. Musical Director: Louis Silvers. Musical score by Robert R. Bennett, David Buttolph, Louis Silvers, R. H. Bassett, Cyril Mockridge, and Rudy Schrager. Art Directors: William Darling and George Dudley. Set decoration: Thomas Little. Costumes by Royer. Sound Engineers: Alfred Bruzlin and Roger Heman. Release date: August 18, 1939. Running time: 101 minutes.

With Cedric Hardwicke

150

With Walter Brennan and Cedric Hardwicke

With Walter Brennan

The Cast

Henry M. Stanley	Spencer Tracy
Eve Kingsley	Nancy Kelly
Gareth Tyce	Richard Greene
Jeff Slocum	Walter Brennan
Lord Tyce	Charles Coburn
Dr. David Livingstone	Sir Cedric Hardwicke
James G. Bennett, Jr.	Henry Hull
John Kingsley	Henry Travers
Sir John Gresham	Miles Mander
Mr. Cranston	David Torrence

and Paul Stanton, Holmes Herbert, Montague Shaw, Brandon Hurst, Hassan Said, Paul Harvey, Russell Hicks, Frank Doe, Joseph Crehan, Robert Middlemass, Frank Jaquet, and Clarence Derwent

Synopsis

Returning from the Indian wars in the American West, Henry Stanley, a newspaper reporter, is assigned by his editor, James Gordon Bennett, to go to Africa and find the lost missionary Dr. Livingstone. After many adventures, Stanley finds Dr. Livingstone alive in a native village in central Africa. Stanley returns and tells the world what he has seen, but many scoff at his story. However, in time Stanley is proven correct.

Review

B. R. Crisler, *The New York Times*

The motion picture which Darryl Zanuck and company have fabricated on the theme of Henry M. Stan-

ley's successful search for the unlost missionary Dr. David Livingstone is one which, on the whole, celebrates worthily the story of perhaps the toughest news assignment in journalistic history. Intelligent and restrained and dignified, even to the point of playing down the moment which brought forth that favorite quotation, "Dr. Livingstone, I presume?" *Stanley and Livingstone* is the best break the Fourth Estate has had on the screen since the beginning of the Stereotype Era.

Incidentally, Spencer Tracy is an equally nice thing to happen to the profession, which ought to acquire a better tone simply from the fact that a good actor performs the role. The temptation to let the pendulum passively swing from the customary flippant-souse to the other, even less bearable, Richard Harding Davis extreme, must have been a great one, but Zanuck and company have sternly put it aside in favor of simplicity, honesty, and good taste. All in all, *Stanley and Livingstone* represents rather a fine renunciation of cheap dramatics by a studio which occasionally in the past has shown an inclination toward overindulgence. Let us hope that it marks the beginning of a reformation.

The life of Henry Stanley, like the lives of many great men, seems to have been marred for cinematic uses by a paucity of romantic detail. Mr. Zanuck, however, has remedied that, with his usual generosity. We do not know what authority he may have, if any, for Nancy Kelly, whom Stanley, it seems, loves in vain, because of the dimples of Richard Greene. But neither do we see how anyone could be so officious as to de-

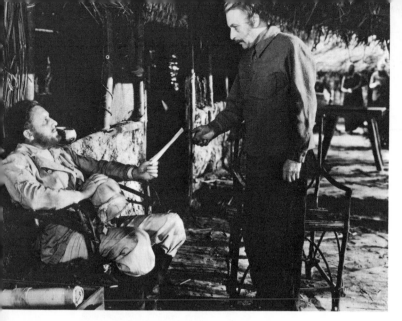

With Cedric Hardwicke

*With Henry Travers, Nancy Kelly,
and Richard Greene*

mand that the presence of an actress so charming, so capable and so mature, for all her youth, must also be supported by documents. Equally, the character of Charles Coburn, as the jealous but finally quite sporting British rival of James Gordon Bennett, Jr., amusingly justifies itself.

We can cheerfully accept the portentous meeting of the royal geographers, and the cablegram establishing Livingstone's existence by announcing his death, which arrives just in time to turn repudiation and ridicule into cheers; why quibble about dates? But the spectacle of Henry Stanley, whom the natives knew as "Bula Ma-

tari," the unswervable, saddened, prematurely aged, disappointed in love—going back to Africa to carry on Dr. Livingstone's unfinished missionary business—that is really too much. Stanley did go back, but he went to carve out a continent and prepare a route for empire; his achievements finally were those of a great geographer, not of an amateur salvationist. Mr. Zanuck's "Onward, Christian Soldiers" conclusion therefore was merely for the sake of a touching finale, and is not warranted by the facts. It seems rather important in such matters that even the cinema should endeavor to keep the record straight.

152

With Hedy Lamarr

I Take This Woman

1940

Produced and distributed by Metro-Goldwyn-Mayer. Producer: Bernard H. Hyman. Director: W. S. Van Dyke. Assistant Director: Hugh Boswell. Screenplay by James Kevin McGuinness, based on an original story by Charles MacArthur. Photography: Harold Rosson.

Editor: George Boemler. Musical score by Bronislau Kaper and Arthur Guttman. Art Director: Cedric Gibbons. Associate Art Director: Paul Groesse. Release date: February 2, 1940. Running time: 97 minutes.

With Hedy Lamarr and Verree Teasdale

With Hedy Lamarr

With Hedy Lamarr

The Cast

Karl Decker	Spencer Tracy
Georgi Gragore	Hedy Lamarr
Madame Marcesca	Verree Teasdale
Phil Mayberry	Kent Taylor
Linda Rogers	Laraine Day
Sandra Mayberry	Mona Barrie
Joe	Jack Carson
Bill Rogers	Paul Cavanagh
Dr. Duveen	Louis Calhern
Gertie	Marjorie Main

and Frances Drake, George E. Stone, Willie Best, Don Castle, D. Frantz, and Reed Hadley

Synopsis

Dr. Decker marries Georgi, who had attempted suicide because of an unhappy love affair, and tries to win her love. To give her everything she wants, he gives up his practice at a clinic in a poor district and becomes a physician to the wealthy. Later, when he thinks his marriage has failed, he gives up his practice and plans to leave on a research expedition. But Georgi has not failed him. She and several old friends help the doctor to return to his old practice at the clinic and all ends happily.

With Hedy Lamarr

With Hedy Lamarr

With Ruth Hussey and
Robert Young

Northwest Passage

1940

Produced and distributed by Metro-Goldwyn-Mayer. A King Vidor Production. Producer: Hunt Stromberg. Director: King Vidor. Assistant Director: Robert Golden. Screenplay by Laurence Stallings and Talbot Jennings, based on a novel by Kenneth Roberts. Photography by Sidney Wagner and William V. Skall. Technicolor Director: Natalie Kalmus. Associate Tech- nicolor Director: Henri Jaffa. Musical score by Herbert Stothart. Art Director: Cedric Gibbons. Associate Art Director: Malcolm Brown. Set decoration: Edwin B. Willis. Makeup: Jack Dawn. Sound recording: Douglas Shearer. Release date: February 23, 1940. Running time: 125 minutes.

With Robert Young

The Cast

Major Robert Rogers	Spencer Tracy
Langdon Towne	Robert Young
Hunk Marriner	Walter Brennan
Elizabeth Browne	Ruth Hussey
Cap Huff	Nat Pendleton
Reverend Browne	Louis Hector
Humphrey Towne	Robert Barrat
Lord Amherst	Lumsden Hare
Sergeant McNott	Donald McBride
Jennie Coit	Isabel Jewell
Lieutenant Avery	Douglas Walton
Lieutenant Crofton	Addison Richards
Jesse Beacham	Hugh Sothern
Webster	Regis Toomey
Wiseman Clagett	Montagu Love
Sam Livermore	Lester Matthews
Captain Ogden	Truman Bradley
Konkapot	Andrew Pena

Synopsis

When Elizabeth Browne's father refuses to let her marry Langdon Towne, Towne gets drunk, talks too much, and is forced to leave town. Towne and Hunk Marriner meet Major Robert Rogers, who talks them into joining his Rangers, about to leave on an assignment. They are to destroy a village of marauding Indians. After a strenuous march, during which they carry huge boats over a mountain, trek through swamps, and ford a river torrent by means of a human chain, they reach the village, which they burn, killing all the inhabitants. Without food, they struggle toward Fort Wentworth where the British soldiers are to meet them with supplies. Dividing themselves into groups to avoid Indians and hunt for food, they find only about half the outfit alive when they converge at the fort. But there is no one and no supplies there. Just when despair is deepest, the British arrive with food and supplies. The Rangers then return as heroes to Portsmouth,

With Walter Brennan

With Robert Young

where Major Rogers announces another and more difficult expedition to the West. Langdon Towne, determined to pursue his career as an artist, decides to remain behind.

Review

Philip T. Hartung, *The Commonweal*

Laurence Stallings and Talbot Jennings, in making a good screenplay from Kenneth Roberts' *Northwest Passage,* wisely limited themselves to the first part of the novel, the 1759 expedition of Rogers' Rangers to wipe out the Indians at St. Francis. Their script, Hunt Stromberg's production, King Vidor's dynamic direction and the convincing acting of an almost all-male cast, led by Spencer Tracy, in another of those tremendously moving performances that win him Oscars, combine to make a patriotic, historical film of first caliber.

SpencerTRACY · Robert YOUNG

KENNETH ROBERTS
NORTHWEST
PASSAGE

IN M·G·M's
NORTHWEST PASSAGE

COLOR BY TECHNICOLOR
with WALTER BRENNAN · RUTH HUSSEY
Screen Play by LAURENCE STALLINGS and TALBOT JENNINGS
Based on the Novel by Kenneth Roberts
Produced by HUNT STROMBERG · Directed by KING VIDOR

With Charles Coburn

Edison, the Man

1940

Produced and distributed by Metro-Goldwyn-Mayer. A Clarence Brown Production. Producer: John W. Considine, Jr. Associate Producer: Orville O. Dull. Director: Clarence Brown. Assistant Director: Robert A. Golden. Screenplay by Talbot Jennings and Bradbury Foote, based on an original story by Dore Schary and Hugo Butler. Photography: Harold Rosson. Editor: Frederick Y. Smith. Musical score: Herbert Stoth-art. Art Director: Cedric Gibbons. Associate Art Director: John S. Detlie. Technical Advisers: William A. Simonds, The Edison Institute, Dearborn, Michigan; and Norman R. Speiden, Director of Historical Research, Thomas A. Edison, Inc., West Orange, New Jersey. Release date: May 10, 1940. Running time: 107 minutes.

With Rita Johnson

"Let There Be Light . . ."

The Cast

Thomas A. Edison	Spencer Tracy
Mary Stillwell	Rita Johnson
Bunt Cavatt	Lynne Overman
General Powell	Charles Coburn
Mr. Taggart	Gene Lockhart
Ben Els	Henry Travers
Michael Simon	Felix Bressart

and Peter Godfrey, Guy D'Ennery, Byron Foulger, Milton Parsons, Arthur Aylesworth, Gene Reynolds, Addison Richards, Grant Mitchell, Paul Hurst, George Lessey, Jay Ward, and Ann Gillis

Synopsis

The film begins with Mr. Edison at the age of eighty-two being interviewed by two high-school journalists just before he is to go to a dinner in his honor celebrating the fiftieth anniversary of his creation of the incandescent lamp. Edison goes to the dinner, begins his speech and the story moves back in time to show him as a young man of twenty-two arriving in New York City. Following the actual struggles of young Edison, who finally becomes successful when he sells his first important invention, the Universal Printer (a type of stock-ticker), to Western Union for $40,000.

With Gene Lockhart and Byron Foulger

159

With Gene Reynolds, Rita Johnson, and Henry Travers

To save his Menlo Park laboratory from attachment, he develops more devices. He invents the phonograph. Then he invents the incandescent lamp, which is soon dramatically used to light the streets of New York for the first time in 1882. The film returns to the 1929 dinner with Mr. Edison concluding his speech, in which he asks "if human ingenuity is keeping balance with humanity."

Reviews

Newsweek

. . . Although Spencer Tracy bears more than a passing resemblance to the genius he projects and diligently studied the great man's mannerisms, he is still more Tracy than Edison—except for the few scenes in which he relies on makeup (a departure for this actor) to impersonate the 82-year-old inventor. Nevertheless, the star holds an episodic script together by the persuasion and restraint of his performance.

Philip T. Hartung, *The Commonweal*

Edison, the Man isn't really a bad picture at all; it's just that the same formula has been used so often with these lives-of-the-great-men films that it has become stereotyped. Spencer Tracy, one of Hollywood's most capable and sincere actors, is well cast as the struggling inventor who works against all odds.

Boom Town

1940

Produced and distributed by Metro-Goldwyn-Mayer. Producer: Sam Zimbalist. Director: Jack Conway. Assistant Director: Horace Hough. Screenplay by John Lee Mahin, based on a short story by James Edward Grant. Photography: Harold Rosson. Editor: Blanche Sewell. Special effects: Arnold Gillespie. Montage: John Hoffman. Musical score: Franz Waxman. Art Director: Cedric Gibbons. Associate Art Director: Eddie Imazu. Costumes by Adrian and Giles Steele. Recording Engineer: Douglas Shearer. Release date: August 30, 1940. Running time: 116 minutes.

With Clark Gable

With Claudette Colbert

With Hedy Lamarr

Synopsis

John McMasters and John Sand come to a developing oil town to make their fortune. They meet, quarrel, and then join forces. Betsy Bartlett comes West to marry Sand, but meets McMasters and marries him instead. Working together, Big John and Square John make their fortune in the oil industry. When they lose that fortune, they come to realize that their personal relationships mean more than the money they made.

Review

Bosley Crowther, *The New York Times*

For sheer and abandoned extravagance, there hasn't

With Clark Gable and Frank Morgan

The Cast

Big John McMasters	Clark Gable
Square John Sand	Spencer Tracy
Betsy Bartlett	Claudette Colbert
Karen Vanmeer	Hedy Lamarr
Luther Aldrich	Frank Morgan
Harry Compton	Lionel Atwill
Harmony Jones	Chill Wills
Whitey	Marion Martin

and Minna Gombell, Joe Yule, Horace Murphy, Roy Gordon, Richard Lane, Casey Johnson, Baby Quintanilla, George Lessey, Sara Haden, Frank Orth, Frank McGlynn, Sr., and Curt Bois

With Minna Gombell

162

With Clark Gable

With Frank Morgan

been a phase of American industrial development to compare with the hectic opening up of our great and abundant oil fields. And for pretty much the same reason, there hasn't been a picture in a long time to compare with Metro's roaring *Boom Town,* which touches upon that dramatic subject.

In the manner of a "wildcat" driller indifferent to the laws of conservation, the Culver City producers have really shot the works. They have pitched in Spencer Tracy, Clark Gable, Claudette Colbert, and Hedy Lamarr to top their cast; they have provided an impressive background of mounting derricks, throbbing machinery, and boom-town badness to get the oily flavor across. And they have come off with a big, brawling, sprawling action picture which the audiences at the Capitol Theatre seemed to enjoy mightily yesterday.

But, likewise in the manner of a driller once he has tapped a pressure dome, director Jack Conway has had some difficulty controlling the flow of the film. Like a gusher, it comes in with a blast, backed up by the volcanic energy of Mr. Gable and Mr. Tracy, who start out as a couple of tough "wildcatters" booming around on the hunt for producing sands. There is a magnificent shot of their first pay-hole blowing in with a mighty roar, splintering the head on the rig, and hurtling a

black geyser into the sky. And there is also a thrilling sequence of the two partners "shooting" a blazing well with nitroglycerine to extinguish the ravaging fire. This part of the picture is high-cut OIL.

But when the story is turned into the channels of human frailties—when Mr. Gable and Mr. Tracy take

With Hedy Lamarr, Claudette Colbert, and Clark Gable

163

With Hedy Lamarr, Claudette Colbert,
and Clark Gable

to squabbling childishly, mainly because the latter thinks the former is not doing right by Miss Colbert—then it and they begin to lose drive and direction. And when the whole thing comes north to New York, when everyone becomes successful, and Miss Lamarr enters as a complicating factor, it peters out into repetitious wrangling along monotonous lines—Mr. Gable is stubborn and fickle, Mr. Tracy is stubborn and loyal—until the two old "wildcats" have a bang-up fist fight and the story is finished with a touching show of friendship in a courtroom. That's a familiar though rather limp place to end a big oil deal.

With four stars in the picture, the desperate compulsions under which director and scriptwriter must have worked are obvious. Naturally, Mr. Gable and Mr. Tracy have the most to do and are the best. The former looks and acts like an oil man—brassy, direct and tough; the latter flows deep and sure. Miss Colbert is a bit on the colorless side as a loyal wife and Miss Lamarr is a stunning but routine charmer. Frank Morgan and Chill Wills fill supporting roles with comic elaboration, and a good cast brings up the rear. More colorful action in the oil fields and less agitation indoors might have made *Boom Town* a great picture, which we assume you have gathered that it isn't quite.

With Mickey Rooney and Bobs Watson

Men of Boys Town

1941

Produced and distributed by Metro-Goldwyn-Mayer. Producer: John W. Considine, Jr. Director: Norman Taurog. Screenplay by James K. McGuinness. Photography: Harold Rosson. Editor: Frederick Y. Smith. Musical score by Herbert Stothart. Art Director: Cedric Gibbons. Associate Art Director: Henry McAfee. Set decoration: Edwin B. Willis. Sound Engineer: Douglas Shearer. Release date: April 11, 1941. Running time: 106 minutes.

The Cast

Father Flanagan	Spencer Tracy
Whitey Marsh	Mickey Rooney
Pee Wee	Bobs Watson
Ted Martley	Larry Numm
Flip	Darryl Hickman
Mr. Maitland	Henry O'Neill
Mrs. Maitland	Mary Nash
Dave Morris	Lee J. Cobb

and Sidney Miller, Addison Richards, Lloyd Corrigan, Robert Emmett Keane, Arthur Hohl, Ben Weldon, Anne Revere, and George Lessey

With Addison Richards (seated), Henry O'Neill, Mary Nash, Mickey Rooney, and Darryl Hickman.

With Ben Weldon

With Larry Nunn

Synopsis

Father Flanagan is anxious to see Dave Morris, the pawnbroker who helped found Boys Town. Again there is a large debt. Mr. Morris complains that Father Flanagan has gone too far into debt, and refuses help.

Ted Martley, a crippled boy who hates the world, comes to Boys Town. The wealthy Maitlands come seeking a boy for adoption. For the first time Ted shows affection for a dog which the Maitlands give him,

With Mickey Rooney and
Sidney Miller

166

With Mickey Rooney

and he agrees to an operation. However, the Maitlands choose Whitey and take him to live with them. Although he is given every luxury, Whitey is unhappy.

Whitey visits a reform school to see an old friend, Miles Fenley, but is refused admittance. Driving away, Whitey discovers that Flip, a boy from the school, has hidden in the car to make his escape. Whitey agrees not to turn Flip in.

But Flip steals $200, and both boys are arrested and sent to the reform school. Because of maltreatment, Miles Fenley hangs himself. Father Flanagan forces his way into the reform school, exposes the brutality practiced there, and has Whitey and Flip released under his care.

Ted's operation is successful, but he refuses to walk. Then the dog he has come to love is killed. At the funeral, Ted finds he is able to walk.

The Maitlands make a contribution to Boys Town to help pay the debts.

With Mickey Rooney

167

With Sara Allgood and Barton MacLane

With Ian Hunter, Donald Crisp, and Lana Turner

Dr. Jekyll and Mr. Hyde

1941

Produced and distributed by Metro-Goldwyn-Mayer. Producer and Director: Victor Fleming. Screenplay by John Lee Mahin, based on the story by Robert Louis Stevenson. Photography: Joseph Ruttenberg. Editor: Harold Kress. Special effects: Warren Newcombe. Montage: Peter Ballbusch. Musical score by Franz Waxman. Dance Director: Ernst Matray. Art Director: Cedric Gibbons. Associate Art Director: Daniel B. Cathcart. Set decoration: Edwin B. Willis. Women's gowns by Adrian. Men's wardrobe by Gile Steele. Recording Director: Douglas Shearer. Release date: September, 1941. Running time: 127 minutes.

The Cast

Dr. Harry Jekyll	Spencer Tracy
Ivy Peterson	Ingrid Bergman
Beatrix Emery	Lana Turner
Sir Charles Emery	Donald Crisp
Sam Higgins	Barton MacLane
The Bishop	C. Aubrey Smith
Poole	Peter Godfrey
Mrs. Higgins	Sara Allgood
Dr. Heath	Frederic Worlock

and William Tannen, Frances Robinson, Denis Green, Billy Bevan, F. Harvey, Lumsden Hare, Lawrence Grant, John Barclay, and Ian Hunter

With Ingrid Bergman

With Lana Turner

Synopsis

During a church service Sam Higgins becomes mentally disturbed and shouts at the minister. Dr. Jekyll sends the man to a local hospital, and there requests permission to test his unusual theory. He is refused that permission. Dr. Jekyll's fiancée, Beatrix, seems unconcerned about his ideas, but her father, Sir Charles Emery, insists that they do not see each other for a while.

Dr. Jekyll believes very strongly that there are distinct good and evil powers in every man. He expounds these ideas at a dinner and further annoys Sir Charles, who decides to take his daughter out of the country to get her away from Dr. Jekyll.

Returning home from the dinner, Dr. Jekyll rescues Ivy Peterson from an assailant and accompanies her to her poor lodging, where she makes a play for him.

Later at home, Dr. Jekyll experiments and discovers his evil self, which he calls Mr. Hyde. Sometime later, in the now uncontrollable person of Mr. Hyde, he kills Ivy. When Beatrix and Sir Charles return, Jekyll tries to explain his plight. Again he becomes Mr. Hyde, murders Sir Charles, and in the struggle with the police is mortally wounded. As he is dying, he becomes himself, Dr. Jekyll, and realizes that death is the only way to destroy the evil Mr. Hyde.

With Lana Turner and Donald Crisp

With Sara Allgood

With Ingrid Bergman

Review

Theodore Strauss, *The New York Times*

Let's be gentle and begin by admitting that the new film version of *Dr. Jekyll and Mr. Hyde* has a point or two in its favor. It has, for instance, one Ingrid Bergman as the luckless barmaid pursued and tortured by an evil she could not understand. The young Swedish actress proves again that a shining talent can sometimes lift itself above an impossibly written role. There is also at least one superbly photographed chase of the maddened Hyde running amok through the fog-bound London streets, his cape billowing behind him like a vision of terror. The film has, finally, the extraordinarily polished production that only Hollywood's technical wizards can achieve. And thereby we pay all debts to the preposterous mixture of hokum and high-flown psychological balderdash that arrived yesterday at the Astor.

. . . Mr. Tracy has taken the short end of the stick by choice. Though his facial changes, as he alternates between Dr. Jekyll and his evil alter ego, may be a trifle subtler than his predecessors in the role, Mr. Tracy's portrait of Hyde is not so much evil incarnate as it is the ham rampant. When his eyes roll in a fine frenzy, like loose marbles in his head, he is more ludicrous than dreadful. When he blows grapeskins upon the fair cheek of Miss Bergman, the enchantress of his evil dreams, it is an affront to good taste rather than a serious, and thereby acceptable, study in sadism.

170

With Lana Turner

Of all the actors, only Miss Bergman has emerged with some measure of honor. Lana Turner, Donald Crisp, and Ian Hunter—all move like well-behaved puppets around the periphery of Mr. Tracy's nightmare. But the fault lies deeper than the performances. Out of ham and hokum the adaptors have tried to create a study of a man caught at bay by the devil he has released within himself. And it doesn't come off either as hokum, significant drama, or entertainment.

With Ingrid Bergman

171

Woman of the Year

1942

Produced and distributed by Metro-Goldwyn-Mayer. Producer: Joseph L. Mankiewicz. Director: George Stevens. Original screenplay by Ring Lardner, Jr., and Michael Kanin. Photography: Joseph Ruttenberg. Editor: Frank Sullivan. Musical score: Franz Waxman. Art Director: Cedric Gibbons. Associate Art Director: Randall Duell. Gowns by Adrian. Set decoration: Edwin B. Willis. Recording Engineer: Douglas Shearer. Release date: February, 1942. Running time: 112 minutes.

The Cast

Sam Craig	Spencer Tracy
Tess Harding	Katharine Hepburn
Ellen Whitcomb	Fay Bainter
Clayton	Reginald Owen
William Harding	Minor Watson
"Pinkie" Peters	William Bendix
Dr. Lubbeck	Ludwig Stoessel
Flo Peters	Gladys Blake

and George Kezas, Dan Tobin, Roscoe Karns, William Tannen, Sara Haden, Edith Evanson, Connie Gilchrist, and Grant Withers

With Katharine Hepburn

With Katharine Hepburn

Synopsis

Sam Craig, sportswriter for a New York newspaper, takes exception to remarks made by Tess Harding, who writes an international column for the same newspaper. The two start feuding via their columns. However, when they meet, Sam is attracted to Tess, and after a courtship they are married. But their wedded life reveals that in many respects they are worlds apart. When Tess is voted the "Outstanding Woman of the Year," Sam walks out on her and gets drunk. Tess writes his column for him, and although it makes him the laughingstock of the sports world, it serves to bring them together again.

With Reginald Owen and Katharine Hepburn

With Katharine Hepburn and
Henry Roquemore

Review

Time

Woman of the Year was made to order for bold Katharine Hepburn. She saw to it that it was: she helped edit the script, sold it to Metro for an unprecedented $100,000, demanded and got her own leading man (Spencer Tracy) and (from a rival studio) her favorite director (George Stevens).

. . . Actors Hepburn and Tracy have a fine old time in *Woman of the Year*. They take turns playing straight for each other, act one superbly directed love scene, succeed in turning several batches of cinematic corn into passable moonshine.

With Hedy Lamarr

Tortilla Flat

1942

Produced and distributed by Metro-Goldwyn-Mayer. Producer: Sam Zimbalist. Director: Victor Fleming. Screenplay by John Lee Mahin and Benjamin Glazer, based on the novel by John Steinbeck. Photography: Karl Freund. Editor: James E. Newcom. Special effects: Warren Newcombe. Score by Franz Waxman. Lyrics by Frank Loesser. Art Director: Cedric Gibbons. Release date: May, 1942. Running time: 105 minutes.

The Cast

Pilon	Spencer Tracy
Dolores Sweets Ramivez	Hedy Lamarr
Danny	John Garfield
"The Pirate"	Frank Morgan
Pablo	Akim Tamiroff
Tito Ralph	Sheldon Leonard

and John Qualen, Donald Meek, Connie Gilchrist, Allen Jenkins, Henry O'Neill, Mercedes Ruffino, Nina Campana, Arthur Space, Betty Wells, and Harry Burns

With Hedy Lamarr and John Garfield

175

With Akim Tamiroff, Sheldon Leonard, John Garfield, and Hedy Lamarr

Synopsis

The setting is a small fishing village in which money is scarce and work a last resort. Danny inherits two houses and woos Dolores. His friend Pilon moves in with several of his friends. Pilon hopes to rob Pirate of his money, but when told the money is being saved to buy a candlestick for St. Francis, he changes his mind. Pilon is also interested in Dolores, but when one of Danny's houses burns down and Danny is hurt in a fight, Pilon uses his efforts to bring Danny and Dolores closer. Pilon even goes to work to help get Danny a boat. Danny recovers and wins Dolores.

With Allen Jenkins, Frank Morgan, and John Garfield

With Allen Jenkins, Connie Gilchrist, Hedy Lamarr, John Garfield, John Qualen, and Frank Morgan

Review

Newsweek

Probably nothing short of a documentary film, peopled with anonymous paisanos, and photographed on the grassy hills overlooking Monterey, could hope to catch all the earthy, amoral spirit of John Steinbeck's *Tortilla Flat*. . . . With much less violence to the original than might be expected, John Lee Mahin and Benjamin Glazer have shuffled the incidents into a sort of continuity for its MGM filming. . . . Victor Fleming, the director, makes the most of its atmosphere and ingratiating attitudes, and an exceptionally strong cast includes Spencer Tracy, John Garfield, Frank Morgan, Akim Tamiroff, and Hedy Lamarr. The result is an unusual film that creates a reasonable facsimile of the Steinbeck flavor.

With Hedy Lamarr and John Garfield

177

With Katharine Hepburn

Keeper of the Flame

1942

Produced and distributed by Metro-Goldwyn-Mayer. Producer: Victor Saville. Associate Producer: Leon Gordon. Director: George Cukor. Screenplay by Donald Ogden Stewart, based on a story by I. A. R. Wylie. Photography: William Daniels. Editor: James E. Newcom. Musical score: Bronislau Kaper. Art Director: Cedric Gibbons. Release date: December, 1942. Running time: 100 minutes.

The Cast

Steven O'Malley	Spencer Tracy
Christine Forrest	Katharine Hepburn
Clive Kerndon	Richard Whorf
Mrs. Forrest	Margaret Wycherly
Geoffrey Midford	Forrest Tucker
Dr. Fielding	Frank Craven
Freddie Ridges	Horace McNally
Jane Harding	Audrey Christie
Jeb Rickards	Darryl Hickman
Arbunot	Donald Meek

and Percy Kilbride, Howard da Silva, and Mary McLeod

With Katharine Hepburn

With Katharine Hepburn

Synopsis

Steven O'Malley, a journalist of distinction, covers the story of the death of an eminent hero and national leader who is killed when his car goes off an open bridge. Christine Forrest, the widow, has avoided the press, but offers to help O'Malley when he tells her that he is writing a biography which will perpetuate her dead husband's inspiring leadership. When O'Malley discovers that the wife could have warned her husband of the dangerous bridge, he confronts her with this information. She finally explains that her husband had become a fascist and was planning to use his public influence to gain control of the country. Her love for her country motivated her in not warning him. She would like her husband's past record to stand for the good it might do. O'Malley agrees not to expose him. But when Christine Forrest dies, O'Malley publishes the true story, exposing Forrest and lauding Christine.

With Katharine Hepburn

179

A Guy Named Joe

1943

Produced and distributed by Metro-Goldwyn-Mayer. Producer: Everett Riskin. Director: Victor Fleming. Screenplay by Dalton Trumbo, based on an unpublished story by Chandler Sprague, David Boehm, and Frederick H. Brennan. Photography: George Folsey and Karl Freund. Editor: Frank Sullivan. Special effects by Arnold Gillespie, Donald Jahraus, and Warren Newcombe. Musical score by Herbert Stothart. Art Director: Cedric Gibbons. Release date: December 24, 1943. Running time: 120 minutes.

With Barry Nelson and Lionel Barrymore

The Cast

Pete Sandidge	Spencer Tracy
Dorinda Durston	Irene Dunne
Ted Randall	Van Johnson
Al Yackey	Ward Bond
"Nails" Kilpatrick	James Gleason
The General	Lionel Barrymore

and Barry Nelson, Henry O'Neill, Don DeFore, Charles Smith, Addison Richards, Mary Elliott, Esther Williams, and Earl Schenck

Synopsis

Pete Sandidge is a reckless combat pilot. He meets and falls in love with Dorinda Durston, who fears for his safety. Pete is killed when he crashes his plane into an enemy aircraft carrier. Pete goes to heaven, where he gets orders to watch over the members of his squadron. He sees one of his men win the love of his girl. But when Dorinda dies, she and Pete are reunited.

With Irene Dunne

With Barry Nelson, Van Johnson, Irene Dunne, and Ward Bond

181

With Barry Nelson, Esther Williams, and Van Johnson

Review

James Agee, *The Nation*

"A Guy Named Joe" is just a title. The story is about a ghost named Pete (Spencer Tracy) who, solid and cheerful as ever—except that the living cast cannot see or hear him—gets busy like the other dead aces, showing neophytes how to fly, fight, and make love. His star pupil (Van Johnson) becomes interested in Pete's former sweetheart (Irene Dunne), who is still inconsolable, and Pete's hardest job is to divorce her from the remembrance of the easygoing, slick-paper love scenes she played with Spencer Tracy. It is, as you can see, a story about wartime love and death, a theme lacking neither in dignity nor in appositeness. Like Happy Land it neatly obtunds death's sting as ordinary people suffer it by not only assuming but photographing a good, busy, hearty hereafter. I am of course in no position to offer contrary proof, and can indeed imagine the general idea not only as believable but as dramatically amenable to very good use. But I don't care to see it so blandly used, as unqualified aspirin, before an audience of which the majority, I fear, believes everything it sees on a screen, nor can I respect the dramatic uses to which the idea has been put here. Miss Dunne feels nothing like real love or anxiety over Pete while he is alive, and only a nominal, ornamental, plot-extending grief after he dies. Pete and the audience are also spared what might have happened if she had really got either frozen or tender with Mr. Johnson, while Pete looked on. So, when she matures

With Irene Dunne and Van Johnson

in her bereavement, every genuine bereavement and maturing which the film by implication claims to reflect and preach to is cruelly exploited and insulted for the sake of what is, at best, an otherwise harmless and medium-silly romance. If you are so generous as to overlook these minor faults, however, the picture will serve as well as two hours spent over the *Woman's Home Companion*. Spencer Tracy is better than the show deserves, and Victor Fleming's direction is of itself, as usual, likeable enough.

Article

"My Favorite Movie Scene" by Linda Darnell, *Saturday Evening Post*

The love scene between Irene Dunne and Spencer Tracy in *A Guy Named Joe,* in which she is wearing the dress he gave her, is my favorite. It's so completely honest and real.

Tracy is a death-defying U.S. Army pilot. He's in love with Irene, who flies a plane for the Ferry Command. She tries to get him to take fewer risks, but he won't make any promises. To take her mind off the subject of his constant danger, he makes her a surprise gift of a white chiffon dress, and later she changes into it from her uniform to please him.

This scene between two people in love seemed to me so true to life that I should think it would ring a bell with any woman who's ever been in love—and I'd think, too, that any man would recognize, in Tracy's tender protectiveness, his own feeling toward his wife or sweetheart.

With Agnes Moorehead

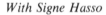

With Signe Hasso

The Seventh Cross

1944

Produced and distributed by Metro-Goldwyn-Mayer. Producer: Pandro S. Berman. Director: Fred Zinnemann. Screenplay by Helen Deutsch, based on a book by Anna Seghers. Photography: Karl Freund. Editor: Thomas Richards. Musical score by Roy Webb. Art Directors: Cedric Gibbons and Leonid Vasian. Set decoration: Edwin B. Willis and Mac Alper. Costume supervision: Irene. Recording Director: Douglas Shearer. Release date: September, 1944. Running time: 110 minutes.

The Cast

George Heisler	Spencer Tracy
Toni	Signe Hasso
Paul Roeder	Hume Cronyn
Liesel Roeder	Jessica Tandy
Mme. Marelli	Agnes Moorehead
Franz Marnet	Herbert Rudley

and Felix Bressart, Ray Collins, Alexander Granach, Katherine Locke, George Macready, Paul Guilfoyle, Steven Geray, Kurt Katch, Karen Verne, Konstantin Shayne, George Suzanne, John Wengraf, George Zucco, Steven Muller, Eily Malyon, Fay Wall, and William Challee

Synopsis

The setting is Nazi Germany in 1936. Seven men escape from a concentration camp. The camp commander erects seven crosses. The Gestapo hunts down the escapees and as each is returned to the camp, he is put to death on one of the crosses. Six are caught and killed. But George Heisler is helped by others and finally escapes to Holland and freedom. Embittered, without hope or faith in his fellowman when he first escapes from the camp, George regains that faith when others including a former love risk their lives to help him. The seventh cross remains empty.

Review

James Agee, *The Nation*

As for *The Seventh Cross,* Metro-Goldwyn-Mayer has used it, with every good intention I am sure, to crucify the possibilities of a very fine movie. Spencer Tracy is a sincere actor and in many respects a good one, but he is hopelessly ill-qualified to suggest a German anti-fascist who has escaped from a concentration camp; very little else in the film helps out, either. In almost every respect, in fact, the picture is an ultra-typical MGM "major" production; it is perhaps un-

necessary to add that the style is fatal to any sort of film except the purest low-ceiling romance. Hume Cronyn, Steve Geray, and Agnes Moorehead do manage to cut a few glints of living acid through all the glossy lard, and one street shot of coarse legs in black cotton stockings, walking with casual peculiarity, has a suddenness, sadness, and individuality which should have taught those who made this film how to create and photograph a city. One has to wonder, instead, how on earth it got into so conventional a show.

Article

"Spencer Tracy" by Signe Hasso, *Movies,*
October, 1944

I think the greatest thrill I have experienced in pictures was when I was told I was to play opposite Spencer Tracy in MGM's *The Seventh Cross.* In my native Sweden as well as in America, Mr. Tracy is considered one of the screen's foremost actors. We had never met, but I felt I knew him well because of the things

With Felix Bressart

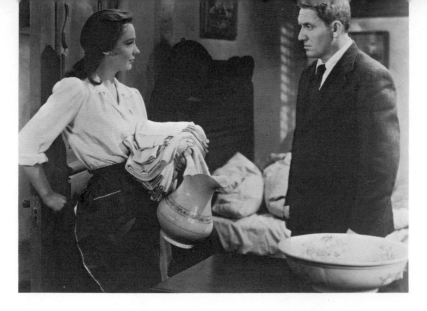

With Signe Hasso

my friend Ingrid Bergman had told me. When she played opposite him in *Dr. Jekyll and Mr. Hyde,* she learned that he was reserved, even a little shy, but that his Irish wit frequently broke through.

Several days before our picture started I had an appointment with the director. When I arrived at his office Mr. Tracy was already there. We jumped into the discussion of the novel, and I discovered at once that, while the reserve was there, he has a way of making people feel at ease quickly.

After work started there were days when neither of us said more than a brief good morning, for *The Seventh Cross* is a serious drama and many of its scenes, especially Mr. Tracy's, were extremely trying. He has little dialogue, and pantomime is never easy. I have seldom played with an actor so engrossed in his role. On the set he was intense and withdrawn, and had little time for chit-chat. During a scene he never went in for frivolous ad-libbing as many actors do. We used to tease him about his complete absorption. He only smiled, pretended to be annoyed, but never bothered to answer back.

I soon learned that because Mr. Tracy is prompt and never fumbles for words there is no tension between him and the actor or actress sharing the scene. Neither is there a question of camera angles as there sometimes is with other actors. If there is a "best" side to his face, Spencer Tracy doesn't know it. Makeup is an annoyance to him. This is one of the few pictures in which he permitted a makeup man on the set, and then only because he was supposed to look worn and pale and had to have a grayish makeup constantly applied to cover his ruddy complexion.

As the picture progressed I discovered that Mr. Tracy can talk enthusiastically about many things when he's in the mood. He is interested in everything—travel, world events, people and books.

He is a great coffee drinker—likes nothing better than to have a cup of steaming coffee brought to him on the set. He is a worrier, never satisfied with his work. And an omnivorous reader. One weekend during the picture he completed several books, including one about George M. Cohan. He says it was Cohan who taught him to stress the meaning of the dialogue rather than the mere perfection of words.

"Read the heart into the play" was Mr. Cohan's motto, and he drilled it into Spencer Tracy when the two worked together.

186

Thirty Seconds Over Tokyo

1944

Produced and distributed by Metro-Goldwyn-Mayer. A Mervyn LeRoy Production. Producer Sam Zimbalist. Director: Mervyn LeRoy. Screenplay by Dalton Trumbo, based on a book by Ted W. Lawson and Robert Considine. Photography: Harold Rosson and Robert Surtees. Editor: Frank Sullivan. Musical score by Herbert Stothart. Art Directors: Cedric Gibbons and Paul Groesse. Release date: November, 1944. Running time: 138 minutes.

The Cast

Lieut. Ted Lawson	Van Johnson
David Thatcher	Robert Walker
Lieut. Col. James H. Doolittle	Spencer Tracy
Ellen Lawson	Phyllis Thaxter

and Tim Murdock, Scott McKay, Gordon McDonald, Don DeFore, Robert Mitchum, John R. Reilly, Horace McNally, Donald Curtis, Louis J. Heydt, William Phillips, Douglas Cowan, Paul Langton, and Leon Ames

With Phyllis Thaxter and Van Johnson

Synopsis

The story of the famous Doolittle bombing raid on Tokyo is retold. Beginning with the detailed preparation, the planes finally take off from the aircraft-carrier, fly to their objective, and bomb Tokyo. Some of the planes return to the ship. Other planes are damaged and lost at sea. The story concludes recounting the travailing adventures of the flyers who crash-landed at sea, were washed up on the China coast, and made their way back.

With Robert Walker and Van Johnson

With Van Johnson

188

With Katharine Hepburn

Without Love

1945

Produced and distributed by Metro-Goldwyn-Mayer. Producer: Lawrence A. Weingarten. Director: Harold S. Bucquet. Assistant Director: Earl McEvoy. Screenplay by Donald Ogden Stewart, based on a play by Philip Barry. Photography: Karl Freund. Editor: Frank Sullivan. Special effects: A. Arnold Gillespie and Danny Hall. Montage: Peter Ballbusch. Musical score by Bronislau Kaper. Art Directors: Cedric Gibbons and Harry McAfee. Release date: May, 1945. Running time: 111 minutes.

The Cast

Pat Jamieson	Spencer Tracy
Jamie Rowan	Katharine Hepburn
Kitty Trimble	Lucille Ball
Quentin Ladd	Keenan Wynn
Paul Carrell	Carl Esmond
Edwina Collins	Patricia Morison

and Felix Bressart, Emily Massey, Gloria Grahame, George Davis, George Chandler, and Clancy Cooper

With Katharine Hepburn

With Katharine Hepburn

Synopsis

Pat Jamieson, a scientist who needs an assistant, marries Jamie Rowan for convenience. The setting is Washington, D.C., during the Second World War. Although they agree to a loveless marriage, their struggles bring them closer together and a romance blossoms.

Review

James Agee, *The Nation*

Without Love is a satiny translation of a Philip Barry play; I like it all right and have very little to say for or against it. Unlike Mr. Barry, I don't find the expression "by gum" charming on lips which use it for charm's sake, and enjoy even less the heroine's recalling, of her dying husband, that he "grinned that grin of his." But a good deal of the dialogue is happy to hear and happier in its skill; Katharine Hepburn and Spencer Tracy are exactly right for their jobs; it is good to see Lucille Ball doing so well with a kind of role new to her; and I have a hard time breaking myself against the idea that Keenan Wynn is the best actor in Hollywood, rather than just a very good one indeed.

With Lucille Ball

With Katharine Hepburn

The Sea of Grass

1947

Produced and distributed by Metro-Goldwyn-Mayer. Producer: Pandro S. Berman. Director: Elia Kazan. Screenplay by Marguerite Roberts and Vincent Lawrence, based on the novel by Conrad Richter. Photography: Harry Stradling. Editor: Robert J. Kern. Musical score by Herbert Stothart. Art Directors: Cedric Gibbons and Paul Groesse. Release date: April 25, 1947. Running time: 131 minutes.

The Cast

Lutie Cameron	Katharine Hepburn
Colonel James Brewton	Spencer Tracy
Brice Chamberlain	Melvyn Douglas
Sara Beth Brewton	Phyllis Thaxter
Brock Brewton	Robert Walker

and Ed Buchanan, Harry Carey, Ruth Nelson, William Phillips, James Bell, Robert Barrat, Charles Trowbridge, Russell Hicks, Robert Armstrong, Trevor Bardette, and Morris Ankrum

With Katharine Hepburn and Edgar Buchanan

191

With Katharine Hepburn

Synopsis

Colonel James Brewton owns over a million acres of grazing land as part of his cattle empire. The opening of the West for homesteading is distasteful to him. Lutie Cameron marries Jim Brewton and bears him a daughter. Overwhelmed by the vast grass country and the granite attitudes of her husband, Lutie leaves and goes to Denver. There she meets Brice Chamberlain, a progressive lawyer, by whom she has a son. She tells her husband the truth, and he accepts it stoically. However, gossip hurts them both. She leaves her husband again. Years later, her son is killed by a posse. Their daughter, now grown up, brings Lutie and James together finally.

With Robert Walker and Phyllis Thaxter

With Robert Walker

Cass Timberlane

1947

Produced and distributed by Metro-Goldwyn-Mayer. Producer: Arthur Hornblow, Jr. Director: George Sidney. Screenplay by Donald Ogden Stewart and Sonya Levien, based on the novel by Sinclair Lewis. Photography: Robert Planck. Editor: John Dunning. Special effects: Warren Newcombe. Musical score by Roy Webb. Musical Director: Constantin Bakaleinikoff. Art Directors: Cedric Gibons and Daniel B. Cathcart. Costumes by Irene. Sound Engineer: Douglas Shearer. Release date: November, 1947. Running time: 119 minutes.

The Cast

Cass Timberlane	Spencer Tracy
Virginia Marshland	Lana Turner
Brad Criley	Zachary Scott
Jamie Wargate	Tom Drake
Queenie Havock	Mary Astor
Boone Havock	Albert Dekker
Chris Grace	Margaret Lindsay

and Rose Hobart, John Litel, Mona Barrie, Josephine Hutchinson, Selena Royle, Frank Wilcox, Richard Gaines, John Alexander, Cameron Mitch-

With Howard Freeman and
Lana Turner

With Cameron Mitchell and
Lana Turner

ell, Howard Freeman, Jessie Grayson, Griff Barnet, Pat Clark, Willis Claire, Winnona Walthal, Guy Beach, and Cliff Clark

Synopsis

Judge Cass Timberlane falls in love with and marries Virginia Marshland, "a nice girl from the wrong side of the tracks." After their baby is stillborn, she becomes restless and spends much of her time with Brad Criley, a young attorney and friend of the judge. The judge and Virginia take a trip to New York City, but shortly after arriving he is called back for an important trial. During a quarrel, the judge tells his wife she can stay in New York with Brad. But when she becomes ill, the judge brings his wife home, where she recovers. Both finally come to a better understanding of each other.

With Lana Turner

With Zachary Scott and Lana Turner

With Katharine Hepburn

With Van Johnson, Angela Lansbury,
and Adolphe Menjou

State of the Union

1948

Produced and distributed by Metro-Goldwyn-Mayer. A Liberty Production. Producer and Director: Frank Capra. Associate Producer: Anthony Veiller. Assistant Director: Arthur S. Black, Jr. Screenplay by Anthony Veiller and Myles Connolly, based on the play by Howard Lindsay and Russell Crouse. Photography: George J. Folsey. Editor: William Hornbeck. Musical score by Victor Young. Special effects: Arnold Gillespie. Art Directors: Cedric Gibbons and Urie McCleary. Set decoration: Emile Kuri. Costumes by Irene. Sound Engineer: Douglas Shearer. Release date: April 30, 1948. Running time: 124 minutes.

The Cast

Grant Matthews	Spencer Tracy
Mary Matthews	Katharine Hepburn
Kay Thorndyke	Angela Lansbury
Spike McManus	Van Johnson
Jim Conover	Adolphe Menjou
Sam Thorndyke	Lewis Stone
Sam Parrish	Howard Smith
Bill Hardy	Charles Dingle
Lulubelle Alexander	Maidel Turner
Judge Alexander	Raymond Walburn
Norah	Margaret Hamilton

and Art Baker, Pierre Watkin, Florence Auer, Irving Bacon, Charles Lane, Patti Brady, George Nokes, Carl Switzer, Tom Fadden, Tom Pedi, and Rhea Mitchell

With Katharine Hepburn

With Katharine Hepburn, Van Johnson, and Adolphe Menjou

Synopsis

Kay Thorndyke, the unscrupulous daughter of a powerful newspaper magnate, loves Grant Matthews and helps him become the Republican nominee for President of the United States. However, his political backers become worried when on a cross-country tour Grant thinks and speaks for himself. At an all-important dinner he is asked to follow a prepared speech. Mary Matthews, his wife, boldly speaks against the corrupt politicians. Grant at last comes to realize he must speak for the people and not just for the party.

With Art Baker and Katharine Hepburn

196

With Deborah Kerr and
Ian Hunter

With Deborah Kerr

Edward, My Son

1949

Produced and distributed by Metro-Goldwyn-Mayer. Producer: Edwin C. Knopf. Director: George Cukor. Production Manager: Dora Wright. Screenplay by Donald Ogden Stewart, based on a play by Robert Morley and Noel Langley. Photography: F. A. Young. Editor: Raymond Poulton. Special effects: Tom Howard. Music by John Woodridge. Musical Director: Sir Malcolm Sargent. Art Director: Alfred Junge. Sound Engineer: A. W. Watkins. Release date: June, 1949. Running time: 112 minutes.

The Cast

Arnold Boult	Spencer Tracy
Evelyn Boult	Deborah Kerr
Dr. Woodhope	Ian Hunter
Eileen Perrin	Leueen MacGrath

and James Donald, Mervyn Johns, Felix Aylmer, Walter Fitzgerald, Tilsa Page, Ernest Jay, Colin Gordon, Harriette Johns, Julian d'Albie, and Clement McCallin

*With Ian Hunter and
Deborah Kerr*

*With Mervyn Johns, Deborah
Kerr, and Ian Hunter*

Synopsis

Arnold Boult plans to make his son a success. Arnold commits arson, goads two people to suicide, and buys off others to get what he wants. When his wife, Evelyn, suggests a divorce, he threatens to destroy her reputation. She attempts to stop her husband, fails, takes to drink and dies. Then the son is killed while showing off. The past catches up with Arnold Boult; he goes to prison and when he comes out he searches for his grandson, an illegitimate child. But he will not find the child.

With Deborah Kerr

198

With Katharine Hepburn

*With Judy Holliday and
Katharine Hepburn*

Adam's Rib

1949

*Produced and distributed by Metro-Goldwyn-Mayer.
Producer: Lawrence Weingarten. Director: George
Cukor. Original story and screenplay by Garson Kanin
and Ruth Gordon. Photography: George J. Folsey.
Editor: George Boemler. Special effects: A. Arnold
Gillespie. Music by Miklos Rozsa. Song: "Farewell,
Amanda" by Cole Porter. Art Directors: Cedric Gib-
bons and William Ferrari. Set decoration: Edwin B.
Willis and Henry Grace. Costumes by Walter Plunkett.
Sound Engineer: Douglas Shearer. Release date: No-
vember 18, 1949. Running time: 101 minutes.*

With Katharine Hepburn

With Katharine Hepburn and Will Wright

With Katharine Hepburn

The Cast

Adam Bonner	Spencer Tracy
Amanda Bonner	Katharine Hepburn
Doris Attinger	Judy Holliday
Warren Attinger	Tom Ewell
Kip Lurie	David Wayne
Beryl Caighn	Jean Hagen
Olympia La Pere	Hope Emerson

and Eve March, Clarence Kolb, Emerson Treacy, Polly Moran, Will Wright, Elizabeth Flournoy, Janna da Loos, James Nolan, David Clarke, John Maxwell, Marvin Kaplan, G. LaVinder, William Self, and Paula Raymond

Synopsis

District attorney Adam Bonner finds himself to his horror pitted against his pretty lawyer-wife, Amanda, who takes the case of Doris Attinger, accused of shooting her husband when she found him in the arms of another woman. It is difficult enough for Adam to fight his wife in this court battle, but Amanda continually must parade her pet theory that a woman should have the same rights as a man, and she uses this argument to win an acquittal for Doris.

With Katharine Hepburn and David Wayne

*With Judy Holliday and
Katharine Hepburn*

*With John Hodiak and
James Stewart*

Malaya

1950

*Produced and distributed by Metro-Goldwyn-Mayer.
Producer: Edwin Knopf. Director: Richard Thorp.
Assistant Director: Bert Glazer. Screenplay by Frank
Fenton, based on an original story by Manchester
Boddy. Photography: George Folsey. Editor: Ben
Lewis. Special effects: A. Arnold Gillespie and Warren
Newcombe. Musical score by Bronislau Kaper. Musical
Conductor: André Previn. Art Directors: Cedric Gib-
bons and Malcolm Brown. Set decoration: Edwin B.
Willis and Henry Grace. Costumes by Irene and Valles.
Sound Engineer: Douglas Shearer. Release date: Janu-
ary 6, 1950. Running time: 98 minutes.*

The Cast

Carnahan	Spencer Tracy
John Royer	James Stewart
Luana	Valentina Cortesa
The Dutchman	Sydney Greenstreet
Kellar	John Hodiak
John Manchester	Lionel Barrymore
Romano	Gilbert Roland
Bruno Gruber	Roland Winters

and Richard Loo, Ian MacDonald, Lester Matthews, Charles Meredith, and James Todd

Synopsis

John Royer, newspaper reporter and adventurer from the Far East, convinces his former publisher who convinces Washington officials to carry out a plan to ob-
tain sorely needed rubber from under the eyes and
guns of the Japanese invaders. To help carry out the
scheme, Carnahan is released from prison. The Dutch-
man explains how they can carry out the plan. Royer
and Carnahan go to southeast Asia, and begin sending
out shipments of rubber. Taking out the third and last
shipment, Royer is killed, and Carnahan, though
wounded, gets the shipment out and kills the Japanese
officer who tried to stop them.

With James Stewart

202

Review

Ezra Goodman, Los Angeles *Daily News*

Malaya which opened hereabouts yesterday, is a top-budgeted MGM movie with a cast of rather mammoth proportions for these days of economically financed films.

It is interesting to trace the development of *Malaya* to see how it got into the works and how it turned into such a vast project.

Daily News publisher and editor-in-chief Manchester Boddy wrote a letter to the late President Franklin D. Roosevelt in 1942, suggesting a plan to alleviate the rubber shortage in wartime United States by secretly exporting valuable rubber to the allies from Japanese-occupied Malaya.

President Roosevelt then wrote a letter to Boddy thanking him for his suggestion and saying that "we are already moving in this direction."

The Malaya operation was a great success and netted nearly 300,000 tons of crucially important rubber.

After the war. Boddy sold an original screen story on the subject to Dore Schary, then RKO production chief. Schary had a screenplay prepared by Frank Fenton.

When Schary moved to Metro, he took the Fenton script with him and slated it for top production. The screenplay was handed to Spencer Tracy for his consideration.

Tracy, who had just returned from England where he had made *Edward, My Son,* was so enthused with the scenario that he agreed to cut his vacation short to appear in it. One of the things that sold Tracy on

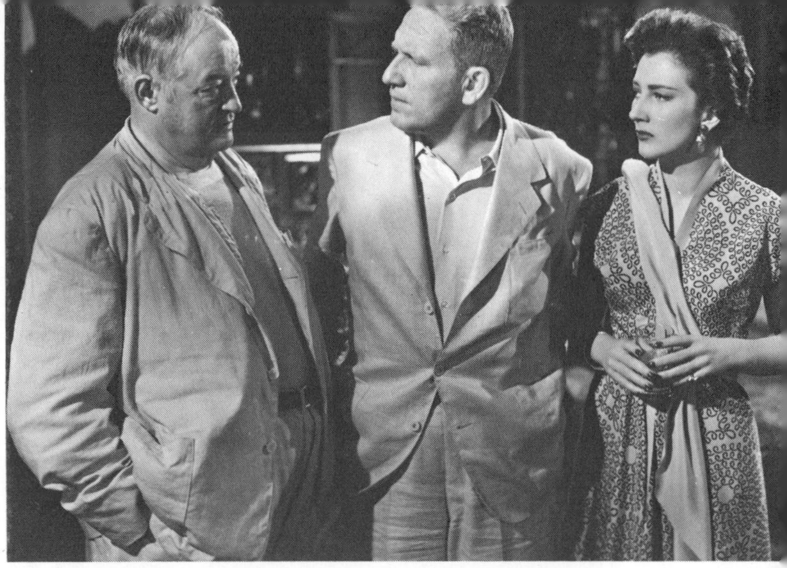

With Sydney Greenstreet and Valentina Cortesa

Malaya was that his role as a hard-hitting soldier of fortune constituted a return to the tough-guy portrayals he once did in pictures.

With Tracy keen on the part, the production wheels began rolling on *Malaya.* Edwin H. Knopf, who had produced *Edward, My Son,* was assigned to the picture. Knopf brought in Fenton for a script rewrite.

Having heard that Tracy was going to appear in *Malaya,* James Stewart asked to see the script and quickly agreed to play the foreign correspondent in the picture.

"Then," says Knopf, "with two big names like Tracy and Stewart in the bag, we got really ambitious. We submitted the script to John Hodiak. He said that he was willing to play a third part, that of an FBI agent, as long as Tracy and Stewart were in the picture.

"With those three names in the cast, Sydney Greenstreet went along with the idea, too. For the part of the publisher, Mr. Manchester, who is patterned after Manchester Boddy, we thought of Lionel Barrymore.

"That role called for only two small scenes, but Barrymore was anxious to do it.

"*Malaya,* by now, had become such a titanic enterprise that we were able to get an actor of the stature of Gilbert Roland to play a part with only eight lines of dialog.

"Finally, we obtained Valentina Cortesa for the part of the Italian refugee girl. We wanted someone different for the role and she filled the bill."

That, substantially, is how *Malaya* got made as a top-budgeted production, starting with a letter that Manchester Boddy wrote to President Roosevelt.

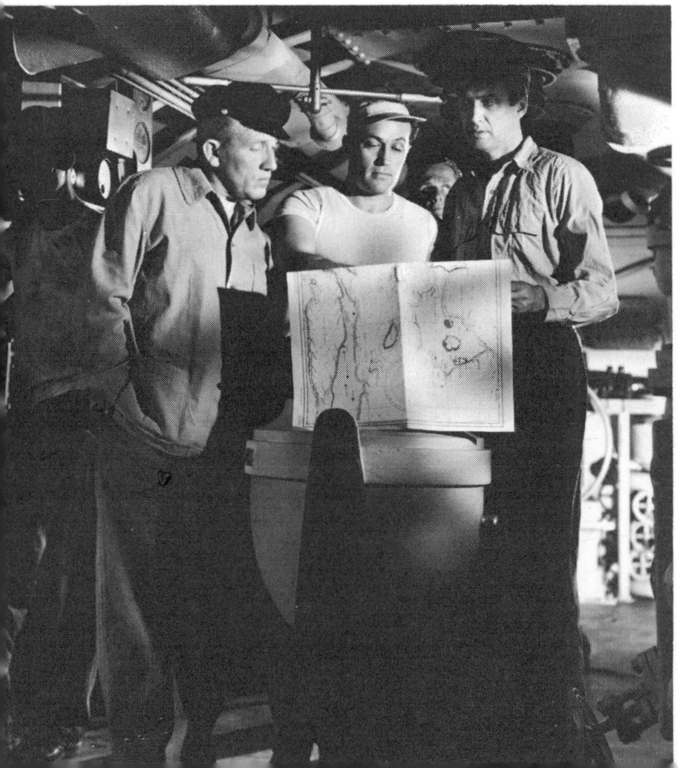

With James Stewart

Father of the Bride

1950

Produced and distributed by Metro-Goldwyn-Mayer. Producer: Pandro S. Berman. Director: Vincente Minnelli. Assistant Director: Marvin Stuart. Screenplay by Frances Goodrich and Albert Hackett, based on the novel by Edward Streeter. Photography: John Alton. Editor: Ferris Webster. Music by Adolph Deutsch. Art Directors: Cedric Gibbons and Leonid Vasian. Set decoration: Edwin B. Willis and Keogh Gleason. Costumes by Helen Rose and Walter Plunkett. Sound Engineer: Douglas Shearer. Release date: June 16, 1950. Running time: 93 minutes.

The Cast

Stanley T. Banks	Spencer Tracy
Kay Banks	Elizabeth Taylor
Ellie Banks	Joan Bennett
Buckley Dunstan	Don Taylor
Mrs. Doris Dunstan	Billie Burke
Mr. Massoula	Leo G. Carroll
Herbert Dunstan	Moroni Olsen
Mr. Triangle	Melville Cooper
Tommy Banks	Russ Tamblyn
Ben Banks	Tom Irish
Delilah	Marietta Canty
Reverend Galsworthy	Paul Harvey

and Taylor Holmes, Frank Orth, Willard Waterman, Nancy Valentine, Mary Jane Smith, Jacqueline Duval, Fay Baker, and Frank Hyers

With Elizabeth Taylor

204

With Tom Irish, Elizabeth Taylor, Don Taylor, Joan Bennett, and Russ Tamblyn

With Joan Bennett

Synopsis

Stanley T. Banks, a moderately successful lawyer, is living a relatively peaceful life in suburbia, until his daughter, Kay, decides to marry Buckley Dunstan. Recounted in detail are the many problems a father must contend with during the preparation for the wedding. The wedding is successfully performed, although Stanley Banks is exhausted by the sheer weight of the problems leading up to the happy event.

Reviews

Newsweek

Working with very slim material indeed director Vincente Minnelli and adaptors Frances Goodrich and Albert Hackett point up each sequence with enough clever detail to make the lack of story almost unnoticeable.

Every member of the cast responds appreciatively to Minnelli's direction, but in the final analysis this is

With Elizabeth Taylor

the story of a defenseless, ordinary man caught up in events far greater than himself, and as that man, Spencer Tracy hilariously sparks *Father of the Bride* with one of his surest comedy performances.

Robert Halch, *New Republic*

It is impossible to deny that the Banks family represents the perfect flowering of the American dream or that Spencer Tracy, Joan Bennett, and Elizabeth Taylor play its principal members with a complete understanding of the rules. But a hidden vice or a trace of guilty independence from advertising-agency dogma would have been refreshing.

Father's Little Dividend

1951

Produced and distributed by Metro-Goldwyn-Mayer. Producer: Pandro S. Berman. Director: Vincente Minnelli. Screenplay by Frances Goodrich and Albert Hackett, based on characters created by Edward Streeter. Photography: John Alton. Editor: Ferris Webster. Music by Albert Sendrey. Musical Director: George Stoll. Art Director: Cedric Gibbons and Leonid Vasian. Set decoration: Edwin Willis and Keogh Gleason. Women's costumes by Helen Rose. Recording Supervisor: Douglas Shearer. Release date: April 27, 1951. Running time: 82 minutes.

With Moroni Olsen, Joan Bennett, Elizabeth Taylor, and Don Taylor

With Joan Bennett

With Elizabeth Taylor and Donald Taylor

The Cast

Stanley T. Banks	Spencer Tracy
Ellie Banks	Joan Bennett
Kay Dunstan	Elizabeth Taylor
Buckley Dunstan	Don Taylor
Mrs. Doris Dunstan	Billie Burke
Herbert Dunstan	Moroni Olsen
Delilah	Marietta Canty
Tommy Banks	Russ Tamblyn
Ben Banks	Tom Irish

and Richard Rober, Hayden Rorke, and Paul Harvey

Synopsis

Months after the wedding of his daughter, Stanley Banks is at last recuperating from the effects of that marriage when he is told that his daughter and son-in-law are to have a baby. At first Stanley is opposed to the whole idea, but he adjusts to the inevitable. Then many problems arise between the maternal and paternal grandparents. Even the birth of the baby does not solve all the problems, but the grandparents do come to an agreement on most matters.

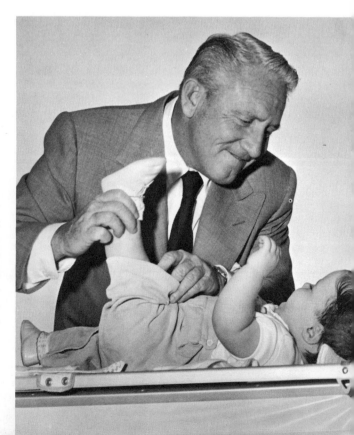

With James Arness, Pat O'Brien,
Yvette Duguay, and John Hodiak

The People Against O'Hara

1951

With Diana Lynn and Richard Anderson

Produced and distributed by Metro-Goldwyn-Mayer.
Producer: William H. Wright. Director: John Sturges.
Assistant Director: Herbert Glazer. Screenplay by John
Monks, Jr., based on the novel by Eleazar Lipsky. Photography: John Alton. Editor: Gene Ruggiero. Special
effects: A. Arnold Gillespie and Warren Newcombe.
Music by Carmen Dragon. Art Directors: Cedric Gibbons and James Basevi. Set decoration: Edwin B. Willis
and Jacque Mopes. Recording Supervisor: Douglas
Shearer. Release date: September, 1951. Running time:
102 minutes.

The Cast

James P. Curtayne	Spencer Tracy
Vince Ricks	Pat O'Brien
Virginia Curtayne	Diana Lynn
Louis Barra	John Hodiak
John O'Hara	James Arness

and Eduardo Ciannelli, Yvette Duguay, Richard

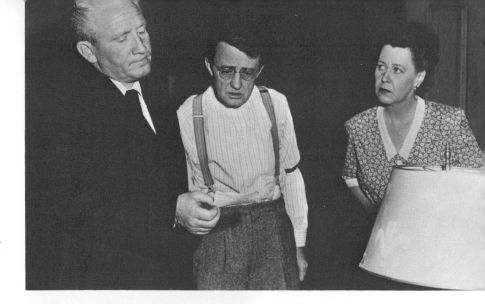

*With Arthur Shields and
Louise Lorimer*

With Eduardo Ciannelli

Anderson, Jay C. Flippen, Regis Toomey, William
Campell, Ann Doran, Henry O'Neill, Arthur
Shields, Louis Lorimer, Katharine Warren, Perdita
Chandler, Emile Meyer, C. Anthony Hughes, Don
Dilaway, Frank Ferguson, Michael Dugan, Dan
Foster, Jonathan Cott, Jack Lee, Lee Phelps, and
Lawrence Tolan

*With Pat O'Brien and
John Hodiak*

Synopsis

Although he had given up his court practice, former
criminal lawyer James Curtayne makes a comeback to
defend John O'Hara. Due to drinking and loss of his
skills, Curtayne loses the case and O'Hara is found
guilty. Realizing that O'Hara may not be the guilty
party, Curtayne sets a trap in which to catch the real
murderer. Killed in his attempt, Curtayne before he
dies gets the needed information to the police, information that will free O'Hara.

210

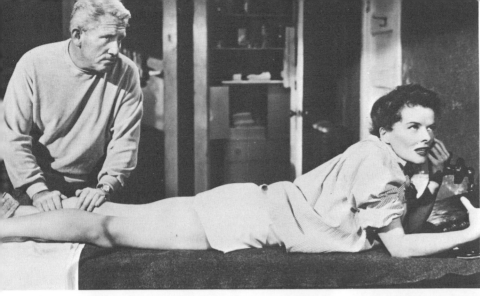

With Katharine Hepburn

With Katharine Hepburn

Pat and Mike

1952

Produced and distributed by Metro-Goldwyn-Mayer. Producer: Lawrence Weingarten. Director: George Cukor. Assistant Director: Jack Greenwood. Original screenplay by Ruth Gordon and Garson Kanin. Photography: William Daniels. Editor: George Boemler. Montage by Peter Ballbusch. Special effects: Warren *Newcombe. Music by David Raskin. Art Directors: Cedric Gibbons and Urie McCleary. Set decoration: Edwin B. Willis and Hugh Hunt. Recording Supervisor: Douglas Shearer. Release date: June 13, 1952. Running time: 95 minutes.*

With Katharine Hepburn

The Cast

Mike Conovan	Spencer Tracy
Pat Pemberton	Katharine Hepburn
Davie Hucko	Aldo Ray
Collier Weld	William Ching
Barney Grau	Sammy White
Spec Cauley	George Mathews
Mr. Beminger	Loring Smith
Mrs. Beminger	Phyllis Povah

and Charles Buchinski, Frank Richards, Jim Backus, Joseph Bernard, Owen McGiveney, Lou Lubin, Carl Switzer, and William Self; also, guest appearances of the following golf and tennis champions: Gussie Moran, Babe Didrikson Zaharias, Don Budge, Alice Marble, Frank Parker, Betty Hicks, Helen Dettweiler, and Beverly Hanson

Synopsis

Pat Pemberton is a physical education instructor at a small California college. Whenever the chips are down in competition, her fiancé, Collier Weld, the college's administrative assistant, upsets her. During a national golf tournament, sports promoter Mike Conovan bribes her to lose, but Pat turns him down. Later she teams up with Mike to do a barnstorming tour of golf and tennis games. Things are going well until Collier Weld reappears and again begins to rattle Pat to a frazzle. But when Collier finds Pat and Mike in what looks like an awkward situation, he finally walks out on her. She finally realizes that she is happy without Collier. The future looks very bright for Pat and Mike.

With Sammy White and Aldo Ray

With Gene Tierney

With Lloyd Bridges

Plymouth Adventure

1952

Produced and distributed by Metro-Goldwyn-Mayer. Producer: Dore Schary. Director: Clarence Brown. Assistant Director: Ridgeway Callow. Second Unit Director: James Havens. Screenplay by Helen Deutch, based on a novel by Ernest Gabler. Photography: William Daniels. Editor: Robert J. Kern. Special effects: A. Arnold Gillespie, Warren Newcombe, and Irving Ries.

Technicolor Color Consultant: Henri Jaffa. Color Consultant: Alvord Eiseman. Music by Miklos Rozsa. Art Directors: Cedric Gibbons and Urie McCleary. Set decoration: Edwin B. Willis and Hugh Hunt. Costumes: Walter Plunkett. Sound Supervisor: Douglas Shearer. Release date: November 28, 1952. Running time: 105 minutes.

With Lloyd Bridges and Van Johnson

With Gene Tierney

With Leo Genn and Gene Tierney

The Cast

Captain Jones	Spencer Tracy
Dorothy Bradford	Gene Tierney
John Alden	Van Johnson
William Bradford	Leo Genn
Coppin	Lloyd Bridges
Priscilla Mullins	Dawn Addams
William Brewst*er*	Barry Jones
Miles Standish	Noel Drayton

and John Dehner, Tommy Ivo, and Lowell Gilmore

Synopsis

The film retells the story of the voyage of the *Mayflower* to the New World. Captain Jones, an unsavory man whose only virtue is his skilled seamanship, hopes to seduce Dorothy Bradford, wife of William Bradford, leader of the Calvinist group that comprises about half of the passengers. Dorothy remains faithful to her husband, but one night she falls overboard and is drowned. To honor her memory, Captain Jones agrees to keep his ship off the coast after he has landed his passengers. For this he is credited with being responsible for the survival of the colony.

With Teresa Wright

With Teresa Wright and Jean Simmons

The Actress

1953

Produced and distributed by Metro-Goldwyn-Mayer. Producer: Lawrence Weingarten. Director: George Cukor. Assistant Director: Jack Greenwood. Screenplay by Ruth Gordon, based on her play Years Ago. *Photography: Harold Rosson. Editor: George Boemler. Special effects: Warren Newcombe. Musical Director:* *Bronislau Kaper. Art Directors: Cedric Gibbons and Arthur Lonergan. Set decoration: Edwin B. Willis and Emile Kuri. Costumes by Walter Plunkett. Recording Supervisor: Douglas Shearer. Release date: September 25, 1953. Running time: 90 minutes.*

With Jean Simmons and Teresa Wright

With Jean Simmons, Teresa Wright, and Anthony Perkins

The Cast

Clinton Jones	Spencer Tracy
Ruth Gordon Jones	Jean Simmons
Annie Jones	Teresa Wright
Fred Whitmarsh	Anthony Perkins
Mr. Bagley	Ian Wolfe
Hazel Dawn	Kay Williams
Emma Glavey	Mary Wickes
Anna	Norma Jean Nilsson
Katherine	Dawn Bender

Synopsis

Seventeen-year-old Ruth Gordon Jones wants to become an actress. Her father, Clinton Jones, a one-time seafaring man, now works at a humble job which scrapes his very heart. Ruth is rejected by a great Boston theater manager, but finally wins her parents to her viewpoint. Ruth decides to reject Fred Whitmarsh, her suitor. Her father finally tells off his boss and is fired. But there is the promise that he'll find work. Ruth leaves to pursue her career in New York City, and her father gives her a precious seaman's spyglass which she'll sell to pay her way.

There's hope and heart-ache in the adventures of a stage-struck daughter!

How To Be An Actress

M·G·M presents

SPENCER TRACY
JEAN SIMMONS
TERESA WRIGHT
in THE ACTRESS

Screen play by RUTH GORDON · from her stage play "YEARS AGO"

Broken Lance

1954

Produced and distributed by Twentieth Century–Fox. Producer: Sol C. Siegel. Director: Edward Dmytryk. Assistant Director: Henry Weinberger. Screenplay by Richard Murphy, based on material by Philip Yordan and others. Photography: Joseph McDonald and Anthony Newman. Editor: Dorothy Spencer. Special effects: Ray Kellogg. Music by Leigh Harline. Music conducted by Lionel Newman. Art Directors: Lyle Wheeler and Maurice Ransford. Set decoration: Walter Scott and Stuart Reiss. Costumes by Travilla. Sound Engineers: W. D. Flick and Roger Heman. Filmed in DeLuxe Color and CinemaScope. Release date: August, 1954. Running time: 96 minutes.

The Cast

Matt Devereaux	Spencer Tracy
Joe Devereaux	Robert Wagner
Barbara	Jean Peters
Ben	Richard Widmark
Señora Devereaux	Katy Jurado
Mike Devereaux	Hugh O'Brian
Two Moons	Eduard Franz
Danny Devereaux	Earl Holliman
The Governor	E. G. Marshall
Clem Lawton	Carl Benton Reid

and Philip Ober, Robert Burton, Robert Alder, Robert Grandin, Harry Carter, Nacho Galindo, Julian Rivero, Edmund Cobb, Russell Simpson, King Donovan, Jack Mather, George Stone, James Stone, and Arthur Bryan

217

With Earl Holliman, Hugh O'Brian, Richard Widmark, and Robert Wagner

With Katy Jurado

Synopsis

Matt Devereaux is a cattle baron who never gave quarter and never gave credit, and forced his own sons to be just ranch hands. Matt makes a raid on a copper works that is polluting his water, but then finds he cannot use his wealth or political power to save himself.

To avoid responsibility and save his property, he divides it among his sons. Joe, the only one of the four sons who doesn't hate his father, claims responsibility for the raid and receives a prison term of three hard years at labor. Matt dies from a stroke partly caused by his other three sons' rebellion. When Joe is released from prison, he plans to get even with the others for what they did to his father, but his mother dissuades him from revenge. However, Ben forces a fight and Joe kills him. Joe then inherits the ranch.

Review

Newsweek

Broken Lance takes a scenery-gilding process, CinemaScope, and focuses it on an emotional matter, the old and peculiarly inarticulate relationship between a father and his sons. Despite a quantity of horse-opera cliché and distractingly handsome scenery, the focus is made clear and sometimes intense by a couple of eminently competent craftsmen, Spencer Tracy and Richard Widmark.

As Matt Devereaux, a self-made cattle baron, Tracy is irritated and frustrated by the arrival on the range of a more complicated kind of legal reasoning than the tree limb and gun holster that assisted his rise. It is a pretty hackneyed role. But he plays it with an elder-

With Robert Wagner

statesman freedom and authority that makes it dramatically absorbing and, at fitting moments, sympathetically humorous. Further freshening all the familiar turns are Matt Devereaux's problems with his sons—the three by an earlier wife, who are unanimously disappointing to him, and a fourth begat by his present mate, a Comanche woman (the deft Katy Jurado). On this youngest son, Joe (Robert Wagner), the father expends a fondness that festers into hate for both in the eldest brother (Widmark). It is a hate that ultimately kills the old man, confiscates the family kingdom, and nearly wipes out the kid brother. To his artistic credit, Widmark—who had worked thankless sixteen-hour days in the family's early, scrabbling times before young Joe arrived on a well-furnished scene—makes such hatred vividly real and understandable.

PUBLICITY RELEASE (Twentieth Century–Fox)

by Harry Brand

Spencer Tracy attacked his role with characteristic authority. In life an unusually definite personality, this part was not difficult from the artistic standpoint, although physically it made more serious demands than anything he has done in many years. An experienced horseman and former polo-player, he, nevertheless, went into training for a month with the roan gelding he rode in the picture, hardening himself physically in the process. When it came time for him to ride "hell for leather" over the rugged Santa Cruz Valley in Arizona, he was ready. He did a lot of dangerous riding in the picture, including a fall from his horse. He suffered some scratches and severe bruises in the fall and

With Richard Widmark and Robert Wagner

219

risked much more serious hurts at other times, but the penetrating eye of CinemaScope does not forgive the arduous demands of their roles. Tracy wielded a bull-whip as though born with it and altogether fulfilled the requirements of the picture in accordance with standards which brought him two Academy Awards and general acceptance as a leading talent in his field.

Regarded with a sort of awed curiosity by the other members of the cast, none of whom had met him previously, Tracy turned out to be a bluffy genial individual and an almost inveterate "ribber." When Robert Wagner expressed regret that he was too young for a certain role he wanted, Tracy commented: "Stick around, boy. We'll age you."

At first, Wagner and the rest didn't quite know how to take Tracy, but ultimately all hands were on a basis of almost continual badinage in which Tracy happily accepted as good as he sent. If Tracy was liked as a person, his co-workers revered him as an actor. Each feels that his career has been definitely enriched by working with him. Tracy responded with enthusiasm for them, too, and at the professional level there could be no possible improvement on their relationship.

Bad Day at Black Rock

1955

Produced and distributed by Metro-Goldwyn-Mayer. Producer: Dore Schary. Associate Producer: Herman Hoffman. Director: John Sturges. Assistant Director: Joel Freeman. Screenplay by Millard Kaufman, based on a story by Howard Breslin. Photography: William C. Mellor. Color Consultant: Alvord Eiseman. Editor: Newell P. Kimlin. Music by André Previn. Art Directors: Cedric Gibbons and Malcolm Brown. Set decoration: Edwin B. Willis and Fred MacLean. Filmed in Eastman Color and CinemaScope. Recording Engineer: Wesley C. Miller. Release date: January 7, 1955. Running time: 81 minutes.

The Cast

John J. Macreedy	Spencer Tracy
Reno Smith	Robert Ryan
Liz Wirth	Anne Francis
Tim Horn	Dean Jagger
Doc Velie	Walter Brennan
Pete Wirth	John Ericson
Coley Trimble	Ernest Borgnine
Hector David	Lee Marvin
Mr. Hastings	Russell Collins
Sam	Walter Sande

Synopsis

The town of Black Rock is a miserable-looking shamble of buildings straddling a strip of railroad tracks on a southwestern plain. One sunny morning in 1945, the Santa Fe train pulls in and John Macreedy gets off. He is a robust fellow with only one arm. He is looking for a Japanese farmer in order to give him his son's posthumous war medal. But wherever he turns for help, Macreedy is rebuffed by some of the townspeople, who were responsible for burning out the Japanese farm and killing its owner. They hope to scare Macreedy out of town before he discovers what happened. He not only uncovers the truth, but brings vengence upon the killers.

Reviews

John O'Hara, *Collier's*

You are not going to see many pictures as good as *Bad Day at Black Rock.* There just haven't been many pictures as good as *Bad Day at Black Rock,* and mindful of the law of averages, I can predict there won't be many. This is one of the finest motion pictures ever made.

It arrives at a time when I was beginning to believe that the movie industry, characteristically, had spent millions of dollars in the development and exploitation of the new filming processes, and then didn't know what to do with them. But at last at least one man knows what to do with bronchoscope, or whichever process this MGM picture employs. John Sturges, who directed *Bad Day at Black Rock,* demonstrates the proper use of the new device, and demonstrates it from the very first foot of film. His cinematographer, Wil-

With Ernest Borgnine and Lee Marvin

With Anne Francis

liam C. Mellor, and Sturges should get some sort of prize, not an Academy Award, Heaven forbid! Academy Awards have fallen into such disrepute that they have become hardly more than attention-callers—calling attention to the exploitation jobs, successful and unsuccessful, done by studio tympanists.

Some sort of desk ornament should also be given to the Messrs. Millard Kaufman, Don McGuire and Howard Breslin, among whom the writing credits are split.

As to the acting, well, at least a gold cigarette case to everyone in the cast. Everyone, from Spencer Tracy on. I'm sure Spencer Tracy has a gold cigarette case, but he ought to get a special one for this performance and so ought the other actors, so that in the future when Tracy runs into Robert Ryan or Robert Ryan encounters Anne Francis or Anne Francis sees Walter Brennan they can always flash the case at each other, the memento of a professional experience they can all be proud to have shared.

You don't often see the oversigned oversigning a

notice as enthusiastic as this one, so maybe it might be a good idea to write about the inside of the picture and suspend this belated valentining.

For the first time in four years the streamliner halts at Black Rock, a hamlet that isn't even a whistle stop. A one-armed man gets off the train—and the suspense begins to build. The inhabitants of this desert patch wonder why he is there and *you* wonder. They are kept wondering; you are kept wondering. You try to get ahead of the script and you decide he is a scientist, something to do with the H-bomb. Or an FBI man. By the time the reason for his being there is doled out to you, you feel no disappointment in having pegged him wrong. Your intelligence and emotions have been handled respectfully, but they have been handled. Sturges and, I suppose, Kaufman have worked on you so artistically, so subtly, that you don't know you've been handled in the skillful way a smart trial lawyer has with a witness, the way the Secret Service has with a White House crowd. You are a victim of suspense,

With Robert Ryan

222

and you are an easy victim because you feel yourself to be not a person in an audience, but a spectator in the action at Black Rock. You feel the heat and aridity of the desert; you want to know what shameful thing is eating the citizens of this town. And above all, you *have* to know what's going to happen.

What does this man Macreedy want? What are the people hiding?

While you are in the theater those two questions become the most important matters in your life, and as you are given the answers you are given them without a phony note. You see one of the greatest fights since Tom Santschi and William Farnum were matched in *The Spoilers*. You see a Molotov cocktail in civilian use, and you believe that a one-armed man can fight so well, and you believe he would use a Molotov cocktail.

In my various jobs—and they've been various—I've known what it is to enter a small-town or a big-city neighborhood where the hostility is so frightening that it immobilizes you. When the fight starts you try to protect yourself and if you throw a punch it is in desperation, with no hopes of it accomplishing anything. Why do they hate you so?—you ask yourself. That feeling is one thing *Bad Day at Black Rock* resurrected for me; and if you've never had the feeling, you'll get a hint of it at *Bad Day at Black Rock*. An actor named Lee Marvin will give you that hint, playing the kind of small-town lout that you know you're going to have to fight because he isn't going to let you get away without fighting. By the time he gets his head bashed in, you hate him so that you wish you could supply a supererogatory kick in the face.

I want to get everybody's name in this piece: Dean Jagger as the ineffectual sheriff; Ernest Borgnine as the creep who gets a beating from Tracy; John Ericson as the sycophantic hotel clerk; Russell Collins as the stationmaster. What I want to do is to communicate some of my own enthusiasm for this picture, so that it will help to make the picture a financial success and maybe convince those Hollywood junk dealers that the good ones pay off too.

Robert Hatch, *The Nation*

. . . It is a tight, economical work, directed and acted with conviction, and it enlarges the stature of everyone connected with it.

The obvious picture of comparison is *High Noon*. Both are suspense thrillers with an evident moral; both center upon the behavior of a man isolated by mortal danger; both work toward a blazing climax through an atmosphere of hair-trigger calm. The new picture is the better by a variety of measurements. Spencer Tracy offers a more complex, contradictory, witty, and therefore more interesting impersonation than did Gary Cooper. The conflict in *Bad Day at Black Rock* is less explicit, and the weight and determination of the opposing forces are less arbitrarily stated than the rather pat duel of *High Noon*. The suspense is therefore much tighter; it increases with the shifting and hardening resolution of the performers and is not a mechanical excitement keyed to the ticking of a clock. *Bad Day at Black Rock* finally affirms democracy, and I prefer that conclusion to the rather petulant rejection of it that was at the core of *High Noon*.

Not that too much should be made of the moral of *Black Rock*. It is primarily a melodramatic entertainment. . . . Even so, the fable may not be too farfetched. We have seen again recently that there is more brass than brains in demagogy, and the inoffensive good citizen may underestimate his retaliatory firepower.

With Robert Ryan and Ernest Borgnine

With E. G. Marshall and Richard Arlen

The Mountain

1956

Produced and distributed by Paramount. Producer and Director: Edward Dmytryk. Assistant Director: William McGarry. Screenplay by Ranald MacDougall, based on the novel by Henri Troyat. Photography: Franz F. Planer. Process Photography: Fraciot Edouart. Special effects: John Fulton. Technicolor Consultant: Richard Mueller. Editor: Frank Bracht. Musical score by Daniele Amfitheatrof. Art Directors: Hal Pereira and John Goodman. Set decoration: Sam Comer and Grace Gregory. Costumes by Edith Head. Sound Engineers: Harold Lewis and Gene Garvin. Filmed in Technicolor and VistaVision. Release date: November, 1956. Running time: 105 minutes.

The Cast

Zachary Teller	Spencer Tracy
Chris Teller	Robert Wagner
Marie	Claire Trevor
Father Belacchi	William Demarest
Simone	Barbara Darrow
Solange	E. G. Marshall
Hindu Girl	Anna Kashfi

and Richard Arlen, Richard Garrick, Harry Townes, Stacy Harris, Yves Brainville, Mary Adams, Jim Hayward, and Richard Cutting

With Mary Adam, William Demarest, Claire Trevor, E. G. Marshall, Jim Hayward, and Richard Garrick

With Robert Wagner

With Claire Trevor, Jim Hayward, and E. G. Marshall

Synopsis

Zachary Teller, simple, kindly, and conscientious mountain guide, retired years ago to raise his brother, Chris, who has become a spoiled and unscrupulous man. When a plane crashes on one of the mountain tops, Chris insists on climbing up to it, to plunder the wreckage. Repelled by the idea, Zachary later agrees to go, rather than let his brother climb alone. After a long and difficult struggle up the mountain, they reach the plane and find one passenger, a Hindu girl, still alive. Chris wants to kill her, but Zachary fights him off and makes a sled to take her back. While Chris is taking money and jewelry from the dead passengers, Zachary starts down the mountain with the Hindu girl. When Chris follows, he is killed in a fall. Zachary returns to the village with the Hindu girl.

With Robert Wagner and Anna Kashfi

With Anna Kashfi

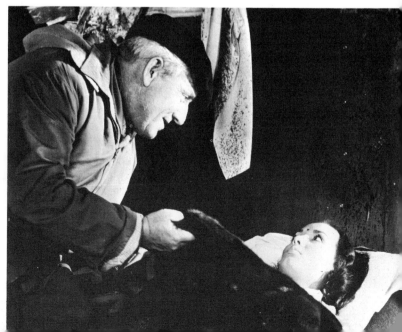

With Katharine Hepburn

Desk Set

1957

Produced and distributed by Twentieth Century–Fox. Producer: Henry Ephron. Director: Walter Lang. Screenplay by Phoebe and Henry Ephron, based on a play by Robert Fryer and Lawrence Carr. Photography: Leon Shamroy. Special effects: Ray Kellogg. Editor: Robert Simpson. Music by Cyril Mockridge. Musical Director: Lionel Newman. Orchestration by Edward Powell. Art Directors: Lyle Wheeler and Maurice Ransford. Set decoration: Walter Scott and Paul S. Fox. Sound Engineers: E. Clayton Ward and Harry Leonard. Filmed in DeLuxe Color and Cinema-Scope. Release date: May, 1957. Running time: 103 minutes.

The Cast

Richard	Spencer Tracy
Bunny	Katharine Hepburn
Mike Cutler	Gig Young
Peg Costello	Joan Blondell
Sylvia	Dina Merrill
Ruthie	Sue Randall

and Neva Patterson, Harry Ellerbe, Nicholas Joy, Diane Jergens, Merry Anders, Ida Moore, Rachel Stephens, and Sammy Ogg

With Katharine Hepburn

With Katharine Hepburn

With Katharine Hepburn, Gig Young, and Joan Blondell

Synopsis

Bunny and her staff of Peg, Sylvia, and Ruthie run a reference and research department for a television network. They quickly answer questions on any subject. Into their office comes Richard, an efficiency expert, who measures the premises for installation of an electronic brain to take over some of the routine work. The girls, of course, take an adverse attitude toward this intruder. This leads to many misunderstandings for all concerned. But the problem is finally solved to the satisfaction of all.

With Joan Blondell, Katharine Hepburn, Dina Merrill, and Sue Randall

The Old Man and the Sea

1958

Produced and distributed by Warner Brothers. Producer: Leland Hayward. Director: John Sturges. Screenplay by Peter Viertel, based on the novel by Ernest Hemingway. Photography: James Wong Howe. Additional photography: Floyd Crosby and Tom Tutwiler. Underwater photography: Lamar Boren. Special effects: Arthur Rhoades. Editor: Arthur P. Schmidt. Music composed and conducted by Dimitri Tiomkin. Art Directors: Art Loel and Edward Carrere. Set decoration: Ralph Hurst. Sound Engineer: M. A. Merrick. Release date: October 11, 1958. Running time: 86 minutes.

The Cast

The Old Man	Spencer Tracy
The Boy	Felipe Pazes

and Harry Bellaver, Donald Diamond, Don Blackman, Joey Ray, Richard Alameda, Tony Rosa, Carlos Rivera, Robert Alderette, and Mauritz Hugo.

Synopsis

An old Cuban fisherman has not caught a fish for nearly three months. Only a little boy still has any faith in the Old Man. The old man sets out and after a struggle, catches a huge fish, which he ties to his boat. But before he can get it back to shore, it is devoured by sharks.

Article

"Movie Log of a Famed Fish Story,"
by Halsey Raines, *The New York Times*

It took six and a half years to bring *The Old Man and the Sea* from its author's typewriter to the screen. It all goes back to one spring afternoon in 1952 when Leland Hayward, visiting Hemingway, an old friend, at the latter's home outside Havana, became the first person besides the author's wife, Mary, to read the newly completed novel.

Hayward took the manuscript to New York and submitted it for publication. The September issue of *Life* containing the story was sold out on the morning of its appearance. It subsequently was printed by Scribner's as well as being chosen by the Book-of-the-Month Club. Warner Brothers financing was arranged for the movie, and Hemingway was given an advance of $175,000. The author suggested that Peter Viertel, whose work he knew, write the screenplay.

With Spencer Tracy firmly set as star, Fred Zinnemann was engaged as director and, in the spring of

1955, initial camera work was started under the supervision of James Wong Howe. One location unit made background shots along the Cuban coast; another, with Hemingway aboard, set off for Peru's Capo Blanco. But only a limited amount of usable footage was obtained from these forays.

In 1956, the production was begun in Cuba. After four months of vexingly slow progress, Tracy became restless, and Hayward was increasingly disturbed by the fact that the schedule was in arrears. Differences of opinion developed between director, actor, and producer. Then Zinnemann told Hayward he couldn't continue with the picture. Director John Sturges looked at the footage shot so far, and agreed to take over.

Units worked at the same time off Peru, Nassau, and Colombia. Matching footage was bought from a Walt Disney collection; other important strips were secured from Alfred Glassell, a Houston sportsman. Another $400,000 worth of equipment was shipped from California to Hawaii, where scenic shots of sky and sea were filmed in June 1957. About five weeks were spent subsequently at the Warner studio for completion of interiors.

The accountant's books show that, with a lavish promotional and advertising campaign, upward of $6,000,000 has been spent on the movie, to date.

Reviews

Stanley Kauffmann, *New Republic*

Hemingway's short novel *The Old Man and the Sea* is a good example of his virtues and faults. The story itself is straight, clean, heroic, and ironic. A man journeys out on the faceless sea, fights, wins, then loses: but really wins because he has had the courage to fight and lose. Fine. But through the story Hemingway, both the Wide-eyed and the Gleeful Exploiter, comes peeping in too often.

It is remarkable how these virtues and faults are paralleled in the film. The director and the screen adapter have hewn faithfully to the story line. This is feasible even though the drama is largely internal be-

cause much of the Old Man's inner conflict is given voice on the sound track—by Spencer Tracy who plays the part. Moreover, a great deal of the papier-mâché peasant grandeur has been shorn away by the necessity for condensation. But it has been replaced by Tracy's papier-mâché performance.

Tracy has had a long career in films as a kind of American Jean Gabin; and although his work has degenerated somewhat into mannerism, a slow-blinking, taciturn competence that is by now predictable and slightly boring, still he has often been highly effective.

As the Old Man, his hair has been clipped and dyed white, he has put on pajama-like Cuban clothes and he walks about barefoot, but he carries with him always fifty films in which he tipped his fedora back and was urbanely sage. It is not the Old Man's personality; and as we often feel impatience in the book with an author who has knowingly "gone simple," so with Tracy we feel that at any moment, having tired of the masquerade, he may reach into the bottom of his boat, pick up a radiophone and summon his motor cruiser. He has not even taken the trouble to adapt his speech to the part. In his casual American accent, the short declarative sentences frequently sound incongruous. This is the closest to a one-man cast that I can remember seeing, so it is easy to understand why a huge box-office name was sought for the part. But, despite the film's merits, the producer has insured his venture at the price of a central failure.

Time

. . . Unfortunately, actor Tracy apparently had other ideas. In most roles Tracy plays himself, but usually, out of deference to the part, he plays himself with a difference. This time he plays himself with indifference.

231

With Jeffrey Hunter

The Last Hurrah

1958

Produced and distributed by Columbia Pictures. Producer and Director: John Ford. Assistant Directors: Wingate Smith and Sam Nelson. Screenplay by Frank Nugent, based on the novel by Edwin O'Connor. Photography: Charles Lawton, Jr. Editor: Jack Murray. Art Director: Robert Peterson. Set decoration: William Kiernan. Gowns by Jean Louis. Sound Engineers: John Livadary and Harry Mills. Release date: November, 1958. Running time: 121 minutes.

The Cast

Skeffington	Spencer Tracy
Adam Caulfield	Jeffrey Hunter
Maeve Caulfield	Dianne Foster
John Gorman	Pat O'Brien
Norman Cass, Sr.	Basil Rathbone
The Cardinal	Donald Crisp
Cuke Gillen	James Gleason
Ditto Boland	Edward Brophy
Amos Force	John Carradine
Roger Sugrue	Willis Bouchey
Bishop Gardner	Basil Ruysdael
Sam Weinberg	Ricardo Cortez
Hennessey	Wallace Ford
Festus Garvey	Frank McHugh

and Carleton Young, Frank Albertson, Bob Sweeney, William Leslie, Anna Lee, Ken Curtis, Jane Darwell, O. Z. Whitehead, Arthur Walsh, Ruth Warren, Charles Fitzsimmons, Helen Westcott, Mimi Doyle, Dan Borzage, James Flavin, William Forrest, Frank Sully, and Charlie Sullivan

Synopsis

Skeffington, the Irish political boss of Boston, runs for the mayor's office. But he is defeated in an exciting campaign. Shortly thereafter he suffers a heart attack and dies.

Reviews

Time

Spencer Tracy is a man of many moods, and he is rich and famous enough to indulge them—even while the cameras are rolling. In one (*Last Hurrah*) of two new pictures he worked hard and gave a performance that may well win him an Academy Award. In the other (*Old Man and the Sea*) he sulked at the director and hardly bothered to act at all.

... Actor Tracy, who bears a certain physical resemblance to Mayor Curley in his political prime, plays the part with more Celtic charm than a carload of leprechauns.

Philip T. Hartung, *The Commonweal*

John Ford has made out of *The Last Hurrah* a fascinating fable about an aging Irish-American mayor in a New England city who's a cross between a modern Robin Hood and Machiavelli.... Moviegoers who expect this film to cover the Boston situation will be disappointed, but they will see a vastly amusing movie about an old-time politician in action. They will also see a superb performance by Spencer Tracy in the lead role. White-haired Tracy makes Skeffington charming,

With Edward Brophy, Jeffrey Hunter, Ricardo Cortez, and Pat O'Brien

234

With Donald Crisp

witty, sentimental, canny, vitriolic—depending upon what the situation calls for. In a way, he's the whole show.

Charlotte Bilkey Speicher, *Library Journal*

Edwin O'Connor's novel of politics and a great politician has had telling and brilliant treatment at the hands of John Ford. . . . Spencer Tracy in a wonderfully vital and authoritative performance dominates this consistently absorbing film. In this case the thinly disguised personality is James M. Curley, former mayor of Boston, who only on September 11 withdrew his suit to prevent the showing of the film, which he had contended was in effect a biography of him and would constitute an "invasion of his privacy." In view of the warmth with which Spencer Tracy has imbued the character, we think the ex-mayor should be grateful.

Inherit the Wind

1960

Distributed by United Artists. Produced and directed by Stanley Kramer. Production Manager: Clem Beauchamp. Production design: Rudolph Sternad. Screenplay by Nathan Douglas and Harold Smith, based on a play by Jerome Lawrence and Robert E. Lee. Photography: Ernest Laszlo. Editor: Frederic Knudtson. Music: Ernest Gold. Wardrobe: Joe King. Sound Engineer: Joe Lapis. Release date: November, 1960. Running time: 127 minutes.

The Cast

Henry Drummond	Spencer Tracy
Matthew Harrison Brady	Fredric March
E. K. Hornbeck	Gene Kelly
Mrs. Brady	Florence Eldridge
Bertram T. Cates	Dick York
Rachel Brown	Donna Anderson
Judge	Harry Morgan

and Elliott Reid, Philip Coolidge, Claude, Akins, Paul Hartman, Jimmy Boyd, Noah Beery, Jr., Gordon Polk, Ray Teal, Norman Fell, Hope Summers, and Renée Godfrey

With Gene Kelly

With Gene Kelly and Dick York

With Gene Kelly, Donna Anderson, and Dick York

With Fredric March, Gene Kelly, and Dick York

With Fredric March

With Fredric March

Synopsis

B. T. Cates, a teacher, is taken to court for teaching the theories of Darwin, which is contrary to the state law. Famous lawyer Drummond is called to defend Cates. Famous politician Matthew Brady appears for the prosecution. Both in and out of court there is a debate between a literal interpretation of the Bible and scientific theories. The jury finds Cates guilty, but the judge imposes only a small fine. Drummond says he will ask for an appeal. Brady, suffering remorse and denied an opportunity to vindicate himself, dies of a heart attack in the courtroom.

Reviews

Look

Bryan and Darrow, renamed Brady and Drummond in the movie, are played by Fredric March and Spencer Tracy. As "the Great Commoner," Bryan, thrice-de-feated Presidential candidate and Fundamentalist believer in the Bible, March struts and squirms as a self-righteous man who had rarely done any clear thinking in his life. And Tracy, with tousled white mane and sweaty shirt, in the salty role of the great civil-rights champion, feints and parries his opponent with a holy light of battle in his eyes. These two veteran stars make the struggle between emotionalism and logic in *Inherit the Wind* as fascinating to listen to as to watch.

Newsweek

Stanley Kramer's latest exercise in Thinking Big is not on the same physical scale as his last—*On the Beach,* in which he not only shook the world but ended it—yet the result is more stirring. . . . He has also put on the acting battle of the year, heavyweight division: Spencer Tracy, who gives a classic demonstration of how to speak worlds even when silent and almost motionless, vs. Fredric March, who by contrast achieves a kind of

With Fredric March

238

magnificence of overacting. . . . *Inherit the Wind* is that rare combination—a thoughtful, honest movie that is a grand show besides.

Newsweek, special interview with Stanley Kramer

"All this talk about making pictures about subjects is nonsense," Kramer said, waving his hand "I don't say 'This is going to be controversial.' I say: 'This is a good story.' "

Asked about Tracy and March, Kramer said: "Those two guys really began to feel their oats, and the crew was fascinated. There was a point when I couldn't hear what Tracy was saying. I said, 'Spence, it's taken me six months to write that line and I couldn't understand what you said.' Tracy snapped back, 'It's taken me 25 years to learn how to read a line like that and now you want me to recite it.' As a result of things like that, each of these two old hams had an audience to play to every day."

The Devil at Four O'clock

1961

Produced and distributed by Columbia Pictures. Producer: Fred Kohlmar. Director: Mervyn LeRoy. Assistant Directors: Floyd Joyer and Carter DeHaven, Jr. Screenplay by Liam O'Brien, based on a novel by Max Catto. Photography: Joseph Biroc. Editor: Charles Nelson. Music by George Dunning. Orchestration: Arthur Morton. Art Director: John Beckman. Set decoration: Louis Diage. Sound Engineer: Charles Rice. Release date: October, 1961. Running time: 126 minutes.

With Bernie Hamilton, Gregoire Aslan, and Frank Sinatra

The Cast

Father Matthew Doonon	Spencer Tracy
Harry	Frank Sinatra
Father Joseph Perreau	Kerwin Mathews
Jacques	Jean Pierre Aumont
Marcel	Gregoire Aslan
The Governor	Alexander Scourby
Camille	Barbara Luna
Matron	Cathy Lewis

and Bernie Hamilton, Martin Brandt, Lou Merrill, Marcel Dalio, Tom Middleton, Ann Dugan, Louis Mercier, Michele Montau, Nanette Tanaka, Tony Maxwell, Jean Del Val, Moki Hana, Warren Hsieh, William Keaulani, "Lucky" Luck, Norman Josef Wright, and Robin Shimatsu

Synopsis

A plane carrying three convicts, Harry, Marcel, and Charlie, and also a priest, Father Perreau, coming to replace a retiring priest, Father Doonon, lands on a South Sea island. Father Doonon asks the governor to permit him to use the convicts to help at a hospital in the mountains. A first earthquake serves as a warning of others to come. Plans are made to evacuate the island. Father Doonon and the three convicts go to the hospital and help the staff and children make their way through difficult terrain to the coast. Charlie and Father Doonon stay behind to hold a bridge so the others can get to the beach. When Harry has brought the others to the water's edge, he returns to save Father Doonon and Charlie, but all three are killed in a volcanic explosion.

With Tom Middleton, Jean-Pierre Aumont, and Alexander Scourby

241

Judgment at Nuremberg

1961

Distributed by United Artists. Producer and Director: Stanley Kramer. Associate Producer: Philip Langner. Assistant to the Director: Ivan Volkman. Production Designer: Rudolph Sternad. Screenplay: Abby Mann. Photography: Ernest Laszlo. Editor: Fred Knudtson. Production Manager: Clem Beauchamp. Music: Ernest Gold. Wardrobe: Joe King. Release date: December, 1961. Running time: 178 minutes.

The Cast

Judge Dan Haywood	Spencer Tracy
Ernst Janning	Burt Lancaster
Colonel Tad Lawson	Richard Widmark
Mme. Bertholt	Marlene Dietrich
Hans Rolfe	Maximilian Schell
Irene Hoffman	Judy Garland
Rudolf Peterson	Montgomery Clift
Senator Burkette	Ed Binns
Emil Hahn	Werner Klemperer
Werner Lammpe	Torben Meyer
Friedrich Hofstetter	Martin Brandt

and William Shatner, Kenneth MacKenna, Alan Baxter, Ray Teal, Virginia Christine, Ben Wright, Joseph Bernard, John Wengraf, Karl Swenson, Howard Caine, Otto Waldis, Olga Fabian, and Bernard Kates

With Marlene Dietrich

Synopsis

Judge Dan Haywood, a retired judge from the state of Maine, is appointed to an American court trying four former Nazi jurists. The four are Ernst Janning, Emil Hahn, Werner Lammpe, and Friedrich Hofstetter. Hans Rolfe is the defense counsel. After a long trial, the four are found guilty and given life sentences, but with the implication that none will serve longer than seven years before they are released.

Speech

by Willy Brandt, Mayor of West Berlin,
given at the premiere
(December 14, 1961, West Berlin, Germany)

We cannot deny the fact, and we do not want to deny it, that the roots of the present position of our people, our country and our city lie in this fact—that we did not prevent right from being trampled underfoot during the time of the Nazi power. Anyone who remains blind to this fact can also not properly understand the rights which are today still being withheld from our people.

It will probably be difficult for us to watch and hear this film. But we will not shut our eyes to it. If this film serves justice, we will welcome it. We will still welcome it, even if we have to feel shame at many of its aspects. Anything that helps the cause of right helps Berlin, and anyone who wants to help the cause of right can also depend on the help of Berliners.

The film *Judgment at Nuremberg,* which will raise a great many questions, is insuring by its world premiere in Berlin that its own importance as well as that of Berlin as a center of spiritual conflict are heavily underlined. . . . I hope that world-wide discussion will be aroused by both this film and this city, and that this will contribute to the strengthening of right and justice.

Reviews

Arthur Schlesinger, Jr., *Show*

Stanley Kramer's *Judgment at Nuremberg,* which will surely be one of the most debated films of the winter, raises the old question of the extent to which movies serve as a medium for intelligent discussion of complicated problems. It is a powerful film, carefully wrought, soberly written, ably acted. It raises issues of great seriousness. It handles these issues with dignity and passion. Yet its impact is that of a brilliant but confused polemic. It has the raw force of an eloquent pamphlet without clear direction or logical conclusion.

. . . As a work of art, *Judgment at Nuremberg* has its points. Stanley Kramer remains an exceedingly able director. He whirls the camera around the courtroom in an ingenious and generally successful effort to relieve the tedium of the trial format. He resists the temptation to use flashbacks, that hopeless cliché of the courtroom drama. Indeed, restraint marks the whole movie after the clumsiness of the first quarter-hour; we hear the voice of Hitler but never see his face, and the single departure from this restraint—the sequence of concentration camp shots—is wholly justified.

With Marlene Dietrich

Kramer also gets remarkable results from his actors. Montgomery Clift and Judy Garland, as two of the witnesses, and Burt Lancaster as a defendant, far surpass anything I have ever seen any of them do before. As the two lawyers, Richard Widmark (for the prosecution) and Maximilian Schell (for the defense) offer brilliant but showy performances. They give the parts almost too much; one feels not only a duel of lawyers but a duel of actors. Still, they are marvelously effective. As the down-East judge, Spencer Tracy is supposedly the granite face of Yankee justice. Unfortunately, he does not suggest that he has been any nearer Bangor than Bridgeport, Connecticut, but his performance is strong and, as usual, falls just short of intolerable self-righteousness. Marlene Dietrich, alas, is wasted in an undefined role.

But the controversy about *Judgment at Nuremberg* will not be over its artistic quality. It will be over its political purpose and responsibilities. . . . It is not fair to criticize this film for failing to solve problems which will torment moral philosophers for a long time to come. Yet, even accepting its own assumptions, one is surely justified in expecting a certain consistency about the impression it is trying to leave in its audience's mind.

Dick Williams, Los Angeles *Mirror*

Judgment at Nuremberg, which premiered at the Pantages Thursday night, is an ambitious attempt to appraise the guilt and responsibility of the German people for Hitler's Third Reich.

The film raises many questions, among them the post-war appeasement of their former Germany enemies by the Allies to withstand the Soviet Union and the responsibility of many others besides the Germans for the rise of Hitler, including United States industrialists, Russia, the Vatican, and even Winston Church- ill, who endorsed the Nazi leader in a speech as late as 1937.

But in stirring up the dead embers of an era, even though we do not want to forget its evils lest they be repeated, producer-director Stanley Kramer fails to firmly fix responsibilities and offers no fresh solutions for the future. Such is the onrush of history that the world is involved in equally critical problems in the nuclear era which makes the Nazis passé.

The picture is well acted, despite several miscastings in one of Kramer's all-star groupings which he utilizes in his controversial, contemporary-aimed stories to provide box-office insurance for his serious subject matter.

Usually Hollywood backs away from controversial subjects (can you see any studio filming a dramatization of the current "far right" boom?) and I respect Kramer for his courage. But his ambition exceeded his ability in this instance.

Not the least of this film's shortcomings is its overlength—three-hour-and-ten-minute running time—in which a slow first half mars the impact of the more dramatic second half. The original TV "Playhouse 90" production of the same story in 1959 carried much more impact and trenchant commentary in half the time. Both were scripted by the same writer, Abby Mann. . . . Maximilian Schell, repeating his original TV role, is spectacularly good, the standout of the picture, as the fiery, nationalistic German. Witheringly, he questions the victor's right to judge the vanquished: "Is Hiroshima the superior morality?" Chief trial judge is Spencer Tracy, his customary rock-ribbed, gently humorous, stern but compassionate self. He is troubled about the trial and makes his private efforts during his stay in Nuremberg to question Germans of the Nazi era. He is an excellent choice for the role.

Larry Tubelle, *Daily Variety*

The reservations one may entertain with regard to Stanley Kramer's production of *Judgment at Nuremberg* must be tempered with appreciation of the film's intrinsic value as a work of historical significance and timeless philosophical merit. With the most painful pages of modern history as its bitter basis, Abby Mann's intelligent, thought-provoking screenplay is a grim reminder of man's responsibility to denounce grave evils of which he is aware. The lesson is carefully, tastefully, and upliftingly told via Kramer's large-scale production.

As the presiding judge, Tracy delivers a performance of great intelligence and intuition. He creates a gentle, but towering figure, compassionate but realistic, warm but objective—a person of unusual insight and eloquence, but also a plain, simple human being demandingly sandwiched between politics and justice. Tracy's gift for underplaying makes the character all the more winning.

Comment

Philip K. Scheuer, Los Angeles *Times*

Which are more long-winded—lawyers or actors? For Spencer Tracy, a lawyer in *Inherit the Wind* and a judge in *Judgment at Nuremberg,* the ideal of every thespian must have been reached: an opportunity to be both. Tracy talked for almost ten minutes in the earlier role. In *Nuremberg* he tops that filibuster and sets a new record of thirteen minutes and forty-two seconds.

This occurs during his summation of the trial of four former Hitler judges on charges of perverting justice.

Stanley Kramer, Tracy's producer-director, tells about it: "It wasn't that we were trying to set any record; all that we were after was to achieve some continuity. On the screen you won't notice anything different. As far as the audience is concerned, we could have shot it in two or three takes. But one-take filming makes a big difference to an actor. Like all powerful speeches this one represents a severe emotional drain to him. If the actor has to do it in more than one take, it means he builds himself up to an emotional pitch and then has to stop in the middle, wait while the camera is reloaded and then work himself up to the same pitch without benefit of lines in order to continue shooting. That's the area, for example, in which a stage player has a decided advantage over a film actor. He doesn't have to stop in the middle when he has his characterization and mood set.

"During rehearsals Spence commented on the length of the speech and wondered if there were some way in which he could do it all the way through. We thought about it and finally came up with the solution that worked. (Two cameras were used for simultaneous

Montgomery Clift

shooting from two different angles.) There aren't many times when a special shooting technique like this is needed. Good screen actors have long since managed to turn their talents on and off as the mechanical needs of the camera require. Spence could certainly have done it. But by doubling up on the cameras we were able to let him concentrate on his scene and allow him full range—where the other way part of his mind would always be concentrating on when to stop and how to start the second take."

Maximilian Schell

With William Demarest

It's a Mad,
Mad, Mad, Mad World

1963

Distributed by United Artists. A Stanley Kramer Production. Director: Stanley Kramer. Assistant Director: Ivan Volkman. Production Manager: Clem Beauchamp. Screenplay by William and Tania Rose. Photography: Ernest Laszlo. Editors: Frederic Knudtson, Robert C. Jones, and Gene Fowler, Jr. Music: Ernest Gold. Art Director: Rudolph Sternad. Set decoration: Joseph Kish. Film effects: Linwood G. Dunn. Sound Engineer: John Keene. Release date: November 7, 1963. Running time: 193 minutes.

The Cast

Captain C. G. Culpeper	Spencer Tracy
J. Russell Finch	Milton Berle
Melville Crump	Sid Caesar
Benjy Benjamin	Buddy Hackett
Mrs. Marcus	Ethel Merman
Ding Bell	Mickey Rooney
Sylvester Marcus	Dick Shawn
Otto Meyer	Phil Silvers
J. Algernon Hawthorne	Terry-Thomas
Lennie Pike	Jonathan Winters
Monica Crump	Edie Adams
Smiler Grogan	Jimmy Durante

and Dorothy Provine, Eddie Anderson, Jim Backus, Ben Blue, Alan Carney, Barrie Chase, William Demarest, Peter Falk, Paul Ford, Leo Gorcey, Edward Everett Horton, Buster Keaton, Don Knotts, Carl Reiner, The Three Stooges, Joe E. Brown, Andy Devine, Sterling Holloway, Marvin Kaplan, Charles Lane, Charles McGraw, Zasu Pitts, Madlyn Rhue, Arnold Stang, Jesse White, Lloyd Corrigan, Selma Diamond, and Stan Freberg

Synopsis

As Smiler Grogan dies, he gives a clue as to the whereabouts of a stolen fortune. Unable to agree on how to divide the loot, each sets out for the site of the buried cash, breaking his back to beat the others. All are unaware that they are under police surveillance. When eventually the greedy parties assemble and manage to unearth the money, they are politely apprehended by Captain Culpeper, old and disillusioned, who herds them off to jail. Captain Culpeper then absconds with the money, but loses it during a wild chase.

Review

Bosley Crowther, *The New York Times*

It's a wonderfully crazy and colorful collection of "chase" comedy, so crowded with plot and people that it almost splits the seams of its huge Cinerama packing and its three-hour-and-twelve-minute length. It's mad, as it says, with its profusion of so many stars, so many "names" playing leading to five-second bit roles that it seems to be a celebrities parade. And it is also, for

With Dorothy Provine

all its crackpot clowning and its racing and colliding of automobiles, a pretty severe satirizing of the money-madness and motorized momentum of our age.

When its producer-director, Stanley Kramer, started to do this film, he said he wanted to make it "a comedy to end all comedies." I'm glad to say he hasn't quite succeeded, but he has certainly made it one to reckon with.

. . . It isn't that Mr. Tracy is funny, so much as it is that he is cynical and sardonic about this wholesale display of human greed and is able to move from this position into ultimate command of the hoard when the parties converge upon it and he is there to take it away. In this respect, Mr. Tracy seems the guardian of a sane morality in this wild and extravagant exposition of clumsiness and cupidity. While the mad seekers are tearing toward the money in their various ways—in automobiles that race each other in breathtaking sweeps on hairpin turns in the wide-open California desert, in airplanes that wobble overhead—Mr. Tracy sits there in wise complacence, the rigidity of the law. And then, by a ruse I dare not tell you, he shows how treacherous his morality is.

Director Stanley Kramer and writer William Rose are saying that their pack of average characters who set off on this money chase are really a greedy, contemptible lot, whose moral disintegration is characteristic of what can happen today, in this money-mad age,

and only laughter makes it endurable. And they are saying that the sensible policeman who watches the chase from afar—a present-day cop whom Spencer Tracy makes anything but a Keystone clown—is just as unprincipled as they are when he moves in at the end and lifts the money from their clutches.

The clowning is grand, the pace is headlong, and the destruction of automobiles is immense. The only fault is the length of the picture. Who can sit still and laugh for three hours?

With Buddy Hackett, Mickey Rooney, Eddie "Rochester" Anderson, Peter Falk, Ethel Merman, Jonathan Winters, and Phil Silvers

Guess Who's Coming to Dinner

1967

Distributed by Columbia Pictures. A Stanley Kramer Production. Producer-Director: Stanley Kramer. Associate Producer: George Glass. Production Supervisor: Ivan Volkman. Screenplay by William Rose. Photography: Sam Leavitt. Process photography: Larry Butler. Film Editor: Robert C. Jones. Assistant Director: Ray Gosnell. Music: Frank Devol. Production design: Robert Clatworthy. Special effects: Geza Gaspar. Set decoration: Frank Tuttle. Wardrobe Supervisor: Jean Louis. Costumes: Joe King. Sound Engineers: Charles Rice and Robert Martin. Filmed in Technicolor. Release date: December 12, 1967. Running time: 108 minutes.

The Cast

Matt Drayton	Spencer Tracy
Christina Drayton	Katharine Hepburn
Joey Drayton	Katharine Houghton
John Prentice	Sidney Poitier
Monsignor Ryan	Cecil Kellaway
Mrs. Prentice	Beah Richards
Mr. Prentice	Roy E. Glenn, Sr.
Tillie	Isabell Sanford
Hilary St. George	Virginia Christine

and Alexandra Hay, Barbara Randolph, D'Urville Martin, Tom Heaton, Grace Gaynor, Skip Martin, and John Hudkins

Synopsis

John Prentice, a Negro, and Joey Drayton, a white girl, meet in Hawaii, fall in love, and plan to marry. They return to her parents' home to obtain approval for the marriage. The Draytons are surprised and then discover they have only twelve hours to make up their minds. John talks to his parents in Los Angeles, and they decide to fly to San Francisco and meet their future in-laws, the Draytons. The two families meet for dinner, and discuss the matter. Although both fathers have doubts, they finally agree with their wives to permit the marriage.

Review

Leo Mishkin, *Morning Telegraph*

With a company of superb performers giving their utmost to the cause, with a theme of direct and urgent meaning for all of us today, and with the same passion and conviction that marked such previous ventures as *Inherit the Wind* and *Judgment at Nuremberg*, producer-director Stanley Kramer, one of the most knowledgeable and dedicated men in the motion picture industry, has brought us a masterful and profoundly moving film in *Guess Who's Coming to Dinner*.

This film is a fervent plea addressed to every living

With Sidney Poitier and Katharine Houghton

248

an important contribution to motion pictures. With fearless directness Stanley Kramer takes a fresh and risky topic, interracial marriage, deals with it boldly, and lets the criticisms fall where they may. The Columbia picture evidences Kramer's uncanny ability in selecting the right cast to portray the characters created by William Rose, to speak the author's penetrating lines as they should, naturally, humorously, bitterly and, in the case of Spencer Tracy, simply and eloquently. The film is the late great actor's picture and he dominates it with his vitality and the clarity and logic of his presentation.

American, as well as a piercing, poignant comedy-drama. In its writing by Mr. Rose, in its production by Mr. Kramer, and more than anything else, in its performances by Tracy, Miss Hepburn and Mr. Poitier, it stands as one of the finest film achievements of the year.

Wanda Hale, New York *Daily News*

Guess Who's Coming to Dinner must be counted as

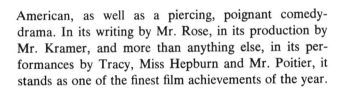

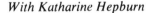

With Cecil Kellaway and Katharine Hepburn

With Katharine Hepburn

At the end of the film, Tracy takes the floor, and lets them all have it. He says the mothers, in a romantic haze, are inaccessible to anything in the way of reason. That the young couple are blindly irresponsible. He presents the pros and cons of the case, tells them of the prejudices and bigotry they will eventually have to face and when he does capitulate he says: "No matter how confident they are, I'm a little scared."

He says a great deal more that makes sense in this monologue and gives a moving answer to the Negro mother's attack on the men for being too old to recognize real love. On this he takes issue and what he says brings tears to the audience, for they feel he is talking about himself as well as the man he is portraying.

Philip T. Hartung, *The Commonweal*

However you may feel about Stanley Kramer's films, you have to admit that this producer often rushes in with timely themes where other angels fear to tread. . . . Perhaps it has been rightly objected that Kramer seldom goes into his topics in depth; and no doubt the same objection can be made about his new picture.

With Katharine Houghton, Sidney Poitier, Roy E. Glenn, Sr., Beah Richards, and Katharine Hepburn

Guess Who's Coming to Dinner discusses interracial marriage at length without getting down to basic integration problems, but it does succeed in pushing the audience into thinking and manages to be entertaining about it. This film is a comedy somewhat like those comedies we used to get from Maugham, Pinero, and Philip Barry, comedies with a core of a problem and a

With Katharine Houghton and Katharine Hepburn

lot of bright talk surrounding it. . . . Someday no one will be shocked. And in the meantime, perhaps we should be grateful for *Guess Who's Coming to Dinner*, which only scratches the surface of the whole problem but is bound to win audiences with its lively scratching.

Brendan Gill, *The New Yorker*

The movie insidiously charms us into ignoring its defects, and for this the credit must go to a superb cast. . . . Mr. Tracy gives a faultless and, under the circumstances, heart-breaking performance. He was ill throughout the shooting of the picture and died just ten days after it was finished, and being aware that it was the last picture he would ever make he turned his role into a stunning compendium of the actor's art; it was as if he were saying over our heads to generations of actors not yet born, "Here is how to seem to listen," "Here is how to dominate a scene by walking away from it." Moreover, the very words that he spoke were written for him deliberately as "last" words. *Guess Who's Coming to Dinner* is the ninth movie that he and Miss Hepburn made together, over a period of twenty-five years, and when, at its climax, he turns to her and tells her what an old man remembers having loved, it is, for us who are permitted to overhear him, an experience that transcends the theatrical.

A Note on the Short Films

During the late spring and early summer of 1930, Spencer Tracy made two short Vitaphone films for Warner Brothers at their studio in New York.

Taxi Talks Produced and distributed by Warner Brothers. Vitaphone Varieties No. 995-6. Release date: June 14, 1930. Running time: 14 minutes. *The Cast:* Mayo Methot, Katherine Alexander, Roger Pryor, Spencer Tracy, Evelyn Knapp, and Vernon Wallace. *Synopsis:* Three incidents in the day of a taxi-driver. First, a college boy tries to win the heart of a flapper. Then a southern colonel is wooed by a gold digger. Finally, a gangster threatens to leave his moll for another. But the moll kills the gangster and orders the taxi-driver to take her to the police station.

The Tough Guy (also called *The Hard Guy*) Produced and distributed by Warner Brothers. Vitaphone Variety No. 1036. Directed by Arthur Hurley. Release date: September 6, 1930. Running time: 10 minutes. *The Cast:* Spencer Tracy and Katherine Alexander. *Synopsis:* An out-of-work husband despondently waits around his squalid flat, while his courageous wife and baby girl try to stir his spirits and hopes. Finally he puts on an old army overcoat, pockets a heavy pistol and walks out, leaving his wife in a state of apprehension. Outside there are noise and gunshots. The wife, fearing the worst, looks out the window and sees a crowd gathering and the police arriving. But a moment later the husband returns. He has pawned his gun to buy food, and a doll for the baby.

In 1946 Spencer Tracy and Katharine Hepburn made a short trailer for the Cancer Society. He also narrated *Ring of Steel,* a documentary for the Office of War Information, in 1942.

Spencer Tracy was one of that handful who have mixed consummate acting craft with an indelibly strong personality—the two combining to produce a unique and irreplaceable style which accommodated a great range, from tragedy to worldly comedy.

CHARLES CHAMPLIN
The Los Angeles Times
June 12, 1967

ORDER NOW!
More Citadel Film Books

If you like this book, you'll love the other titles in the award-winning Citadel Film Series. From James Stewart to Moe Howard and The Three Stooges, Woody Allen to John Wayne, The Citadel Film Series is America's largest and oldest film book library.

With more than 150 titles--and more on the way!--Citadel Film Books make perfect gifts for a loved one, a friend, or best of all, yourself!

A complete listing of the Citadel Film Series appears below.
If you know what books you want, why not order now!
It's easy! Just call 1-800-447-BOOK and have your MasterCard or Visa ready.

STARS
Alan Ladd
Barbra Streisand: First Decade
Barbra Streisand: Second
 Decade
Bela Lugosi
Bette Davis
Boris Karloff
The Bowery Boys
Buster Keaton
Carole Lombard
Cary Grant
Charles Bronson
Charlie Chaplin
Clark Gable
Clint Eastwood
Curly
Dustin Hoffman
Edward G. Robinson
Elizabeth Taylor
Elvis Presley
Errol Flynn
Frank Sinatra
Gary Cooper
Gene Kelly
Gina Lollobrigida
Gloria Swanson
Gregory Peck
Greta Garbo
Henry Fonda
Humphrey Bogart
Ingrid Bergman
Jack Lemmon
Jack Nicholson
James Cagney
James Dean: Behind the Scene
Jane Fonda
Jeanette MacDonald & Nelson
 Eddy
Joan Crawford

John Wayne Films
John Wayne Reference Book
John Wayne Scrapbook
Judy Garland
Katharine Hepburn
Kirk Douglas
Laurel & Hardy
Lauren Bacall
Laurence Olivier
Mae West
Marilyn Monroe
Marlene Dietrich
Marlon Brando
Marx Brothers
Moe Howard & the Three
 Stooges
Norma Shearer
Olivia de Havilland
Orson Welles
Paul Newman
Peter Lorre
Rita Hayworth
Robert De Niro
Robert Redford
Sean Connery
Sexbomb: Jayne Mansfield
Shirley MacLaine
Shirley Temple
The Sinatra Scrapbook
Spencer Tracy
Steve McQueen
Three Stooges Scrapbook
Warren Beatty
W.C. Fields
William Holden
William Powell
A Wonderful Life: James Stewart
DIRECTORS
Alfred Hitchcock
Cecil B. DeMille

Federico Fellini
Frank Capra
John Ford
John Huston
Woody Allen
GENRE
Bad Guys
Black Hollywood
Black Hollywood: From 1970 to
 Today
Classics of the Gangster Film
Classics of the Horror Film
Divine Images: Jesus on Screen
Early Classics of Foreign Film
Great French Films
Great German Films
Great Romantic Films
Great Science Fiction Films
Harry Warren & the Hollywood
 Musical
Hispanic Hollywood: The Latins
 in Motion Pictures
The Hollywood Western
The Incredible World of 007
The Jewish Image in American
 Film
The Lavender Screen: The Gay
 and Lesbian Films
Martial Arts Movies
The Modern Horror Film
More Classics of the Horror Film
Movie Psychos & Madmen
Our Huckleberry Friend: Johnny
 Mercer
Second Feature: "B" Films
They Sang! They Danced! They
 Romanced!: Hollywood
 Musicals
Thrillers
The West That Never Was

Words and Shadows: Literature
 on the Screen
DECADE
Classics of the Silent Screen
Films of the Twenties
Films of the Thirties
More Films of the 30's
Films of the Forties
Films of the Fifties
Lost Films of the 50's
Films of the Sixties
Films of the Seventies
Films of the Eighties
SPECIAL INTEREST
America on the Rerun
Bugsy (Illustrated screenplay)
Comic Support
Dick Tracy
Favorite Families of TV
Film Flubs
Film Flubs: The Sequel
First Films
Forgotten Films to Remember
Hollywood Cheesecake
Hollywood's Hollywood
Howard Hughes in Hollywood
More Character People
The Nightmare Never Ends:
 Freddy Krueger & "A Night-
 mare on Elm Street"
The "Northern Exposure" Book
The "Quantum Leap" Book
Sex In the Movies
Sherlock Holmes
Son of Film Flubs
Those Glorious Glamour Years
Who Is That?: Familiar Faces and
 Forgotten Names
"You Ain't Heard Nothin' Yet!"

For a free full-color brochure describing the Citadel Film Series in depth, call 1-800-447-BOOK; or send your name and address to Citadel Film Books, Dept. 1038, 120 Enterprise Ave., Secaucus, NJ 07094.